• MASTERING THE BASICS •

Pies, Tarts and Pastries

• MASTERING THE BASICS •

Pies, Tarts & Pastries

Basics to Brilliance
Techniques, Tips and Trusted Recipes

MURDOCH BOOKS

Contents

Introduction

Pastry can be the much-loved though problematic child of many a baker. On the one hand, it seems a miracle that some flour, some shortening and a blast of heat can form the base for such a varied and delicious range of food. On the other, these raw materials may be temperamental and difficult, driving you mad if your attempts aren't successful. Do not despair, help is at hand. In the following pages we have fool-proof methods, along with step-by-step photography, to guide you through the adventure of home-made pastry. We also have scrumptious recipes for fillings, both savoury and sweet, which will have you embracing pastry-making. From Snapper pie to Strawberry, rhubarb and vanilla mille feuille, *Mastering the Basics: Pies, Tarts & Pastries* will provide you with the skills and inspiration to unleash your inner pastry chef.

Basics

Common ingredients

Baking powder is a leavener that is sometimes used in quick breads to help aerate them. It is a combination of bicarbonate of soda (baking soda), cream of tartar (or other acidic powder) and usually cornflour (cornstarch) or rice flour (to absorb moisture). To make your own, combine ½ teaspoon cream of tartar, ½ teaspoon cornflour and ¼ teaspoon bicarbonate of soda to replace 1 teaspoon of commercial baking powder. Almost all baking powders sold are 'double acting', which means they are partly activated by liquid and partly by heat.

Bicarbonate of soda, also called baking soda, is a component of baking powder and a leavener in its own right. It is activated with the aid of an acid, so used in mixtures with an acidic ingredient such as buttermilk or yoghurt. It is important to cook these mixtures as soon as possible, because bicarbonate of soda is activated as soon as it comes into contact with the acidic ingredient — if the mixture is left to sit, it won't rise properly and the end product will have a coarser, more open texture.

Butter is the most commonly used fat when making pastries. It adds flavour, shortness/tenderness and colour. Some pastries contain butter that has been 'rubbed in' while others are 'laminated' with butter. Unsalted butter is sweeter than salted and gives you more control over the amount of salt in your pies and pastries — you can then add as much as you want. Some pastries, especially those that require 'rubbing in', need chilled butter while other pastries require slightly softened butter.

Buttermilk is made by adding souring agents to milk. It is used in conjunction with bicarbonate of soda, in goods such as soda bread and scones. Its acidity reacts with the alkaline properties of the soda to provide a particularly good lift. To make your own buttermilk, add 1 tablespoon of lemon juice to 300 ml (10½ fl oz) of regular milk.

Eggs enrich, give structure, bind, lighten, tenderise and add flavour to certain pastries and breads. Store them, pointed end down, in their original carton in the refrigerator. Always bring eggs to room temperature before using — if you're short on time, you can put them in a bowl of lukewarm water for 10 minutes. All recipes in this book use 59/60 g (2¼ oz) eggs.

Flour provides the basic structure for all pastries. Wheat flour is the most commonly used flour. The gluten in wheat flour gives the strength, elasticity and structure necessary for baking. It forms a strand-like network that traps air and assists with rising. Self-raising flour is simply plain (all-purpose) flour with baking powder added. To make your own, add 2 teaspoons baking powder to every 150 g (5½ oz/1 cup) plain flour. Sift them together several times before using.

Natural vanilla extract and vanilla essence are concentrated flavours derived from vanilla bean pods. Buy pure essence or extract and avoid those labelled with 'artificial' or 'imitation' as they are simply flavourings based on alcohol. Thick vanilla bean paste is also available and is a convenient way of adding vanilla seeds to baking without having to scrape them from the pod. If using vanilla beans, wash and dry the pod thoroughly after use and place in a container of sugar to subtly flavour it.

Salt enhances the flavour of baked goods. In bread making it does even more, making the dough stronger and less sticky, regulating the activity of the yeast so it grows at a more consistent rate, and affecting the overall texture of the bread. Salt also attracts moisture, so it helps prevent loaves becoming stale, especially in dry weather.

Sugar is an important ingredient in pastry and bread making as it adds sweetness, flavour, moisture and tenderness. There are several types and the most widely used in baking is white — granulated, caster (superfine) or icing (confectioners'). Granulated is the most commonly available, but caster sugar, with its fine grains that dissolve quickly, is a better choice when baking. Icing sugar is powdered white sugar and is available as pure icing sugar or icing sugar mixture, which has a little cornflour (cornstarch) added to prevent lumps. Brown sugar, sometimes called light brown sugar, is fine, granulated sugar with molasses added to enrich the flavour. Dark brown sugar has even more molasses added. If you want to substitute brown sugar for white, or vice versa, measure out the same weight, rather than volume.

Yeast is a biological (naturally occurring) rising agent. Dried yeast is available in sachets or small containers from supermarkets in the baking section. Fresh (compressed) yeast is available from selected health food stores and delicatessens. Fresh yeast needs to be activated by mixing with a lukewarm liquid before adding it to other ingredients, while dried yeast can be added directly to the remaining ingredients. Although it is not strictly necessary, we advise activating dried yeast to ensure it is still alive. Instant dried yeast is completely interchangeable with active dried yeast, another form of dried yeast that does require activation.

Common equipment

Ovens

Not all ovens cook in the same way so it is important to get to know your oven and make your own adjustments to recipes if necessary. Even when an oven is accurately calibrated its temperature may be slightly out. Use a good-quality oven thermometer to monitor the temperature regularly and make sure the seals are in good order to prevent heat escaping.

Fan-forced or convection ovens, which use a fan to circulate the heat, cook at a higher temperature and more quickly than conventional ovens. The recipes in this book have been tested in conventional ovens — if cooking in a fan-forced oven, decrease the oven temperature by 20°C (68°F) and check regularly towards the end of cooking as the time may need to be reduced by 10–20 per cent.

When baking in a conventional oven, place breads and pastries in the centre of the oven and if you have multiple trays, swap them around halfway through cooking to ensure even cooking. If you have two loaves of bread in the oven at once, make sure there is plenty of room between them to allow the heat to circulate evenly.

Measuring

Careful, accurate measuring, whether by weight or volume, is essential for success when making breads and pastries. Always use one set of measurements when preparing a recipe — metric (grams and ml) or imperial (oz and fl oz) by weighing, or measuring by volume (cups).

Measuring cups are used to measure dry or non-liquid ingredients. They are generally available in plastic or metal and in sets of 60 ml (2 fl oz/¼ cup), 80 ml (2½ fl oz/⅓ cup), 125 ml (4 fl oz/½ cup) and 250 ml (9 fl oz/1 cup) measures. Spoon the ingredient into the cup until heaped, then, without compressing it, run a flat-bladed knife across the top to level. All cup measures in this book are level, not heaped.

Measuring jugs are used to measure liquids. Look for a glass or see-through jug with clear markings and a good spout.

DIGITAL TIMER Count Down/Up
RESET
SEC
START/STOP
Breville

Measuring spoons are used to measure small amounts of both dry and liquid ingredients. They are available in sets that generally include a ¼ teaspoon, ½ teaspoon, 1 teaspoon and 1 tablespoon. One teaspoon equals 5 ml in volume. Tablespoons, however, can come in either 15 ml (½ fl oz/ 3 teaspoon) or 20 ml (¾ fl oz/4 teaspoon) volumes. This book uses 20 ml tablespoons. Check your tablespoon volume and if you are using a 15 ml tablespoon, add an extra teaspoon for every tablespoon of the ingredient specified in the recipe. This is particularly important for ingredients such as baking powder and bicarbonate of soda (baking soda). All tablespoon and teaspoon measures in this book are level — use a flat-bladed knife to level ingredients, as for cup measures.

Scales, electronic versions in particular, are the most accurate way of measuring dry ingredients, such as flour or sugar, and non-liquid, soft ingredients, such as yoghurt or jam. Electronic scales are now affordable and are an invaluable addition to your kitchen. Most give metric and imperial weights, and let you switch between the two. They may also let you 'zero' the reading so you can measure several ingredients in the same bowl one after another, which is handy for one-bowl mixes.

Mixing

Bowls are fundamental to making breads and pastries and it is important to have a good selection of sizes. Stainless-steel bowls are versatile and durable and are good conductors of heat and cold. Ceramic and glass bowls are sturdy and are also suitable for heating and melting ingredients. Plastic bowls aren't a good choice for mixing as they absorb flavours and become greasy over time.

Electric mixers can be hand-held or mounted on a stand. Hand-held beaters have detachable beaters and sometimes whisk attachments. They are relatively inexpensive, store easily and can be used to whisk or beat mixtures, particularly small quantities. They are also needed if whisking or beating a mixture over a saucepan of simmering water. However, they aren't suitable for heavy-duty mixing and are not as efficient as the stand versions.

Stand mixers have a bowl that screws into the stand and usually come with a range of attachments such as a beating paddle, whisk and dough hook. Like hand-held beaters, they have a range of speeds, but their motors are more powerful and therefore able to cope with larger and thicker mixtures. Some doughs that are very soft, such as brioche dough, are easier to make in a machine than they are by hand.

Food processors have many uses when baking, from finely chopping ingredients to making pastry and quick breads. Take care when processing pastry and quick bread doughs once the liquid has been added, as it is easy to overprocess them, causing toughness and shrinkage in the finished product. As flour's ability to absorb liquid can be affected by the weather, the batch of flour and other components, it's harder to judge whether dough needs more liquid or flour when you can't feel it. You really need to use your hands for this.

Again, buy the best quality food processor you can afford, and ensure it has a large bowl. A separate mini food processor that will efficiently cope with small quantities of nuts, herbs and spices is also a good investment.

Bakers' friends

Baking beads/weights are small re-usable ceramic or metal weights that are used when blind baking pastry. You can use dried beans or rice instead, but proper weights are handy.

Cake testers are thin metal or bamboo skewers. Metal ones are available from kitchenware stores and some supermarkets and are the best option as they won't leave large holes in your baking. The skewer is inserted into the centre of a cake or enriched bread and if it's cooked, it will be clean when withdrawn (unless otherwise stated in the recipe).

Large metal spoons are useful for folding dry ingredients into a mixture or folding in whisked egg whites without losing the incorporated air.

Oven thermometers are important kitchen gadgets. Not all ovens are calibrated and are likely to be at least a couple of degrees out. 'Hot spots' are also common. A thermometer will allow you to check if your oven is accurate and adjust the temperature if necessary. Move the thermometer around in the oven when set at the same temperature and note the reading to check if you have any 'hot spots'. There is no need to remove it from your oven between oven uses.

Palette knives can be bought in various sizes and degrees of flexibility. They have a thin flat blade with a rounded end that makes them useful for spreading fillings over doughs and lifting cooked pastries off baking trays and out of muffin tins.

Pastry brushes have natural, nylon or silicone bristles and are used to glaze tarts with sugary mixtures, brush egg washes onto pastries and doughs, and grease cake tins. It is a good idea to have a few brushes of varying sizes. Make sure you wash and dry them thoroughly before storing. Avoid cheaper brushes as they tend to shed their bristles.

Rolling pins should be straight, solid and long enough to roll out a full quantity of pastry or dough without marking the surface with the ends. A good size is about 45 cm (17¾ inches) long and 5 cm (2 inches) in diameter. Wood is preferable to ceramic or marble, as it can hold a fine layer of flour on its surface that will help prevent the pastry or dough sticking. The best ones are made of hard wood with a close grain and very smooth finish. Clean it by wiping with a damp cloth — never immerse a wooden rolling pin in water.

Ruler Keep a ruler or measuring tape in your utensil drawer for checking tin or dish dimensions or checking the thickness of pastry. All tin and dish dimensions in this book are measured from the base, with the exception of kugelhopf tins, which are best measured across the top.

Sieves are used to sift flour to help incorporate air, to combine ingredients evenly, such as flour and cocoa powder or baking powder, and to dust flour onto a work surface before rolling out pastry or kneading dough. They are also used to dust icing (confectioners') sugar or cocoa over baked goods.

Spatulas can be made of silicone, rubber or plastic. Silicone and rubber ones are more flexible, however rubber ones tend to absorb colours and flavours more readily. Spatulas are used for folding and combining mixtures and scraping mixtures from bowls and food processors. Those with spoon-shaped ends are also good for spooning mixtures into tins. Have a few different sizes and shapes for various tasks.

Timers are necessary for accurate timing and to prevent food burning. Digital timers are more accurate than mechanical ones. Many ovens have inbuilt timers.

Whisks are used to incorporate air into a mixture, remove lumps and combine liquid mixtures, such as eggs and oil. They come in all shapes and sizes — a large and small wire balloon whisk will usually cover all required tasks.

Wooden spoons are used to mix, beat and stir. They are particularly good for mixtures being heated in a saucepan and 'heavier' mixtures that require stirring or beating.

Shortcrust pastry

A very high butter content and the addition of egg yolk gives shortcrust pastry and sweet shortcrust pastry the characteristic melt-in-the-mouth texture and rich flavour. These pastries aren't difficult to master, but there are a few basic rules to note when making them. The pastry should be kept as cool as possible at every stage of the process – if it becomes too warm at any point, the finished result will be heavy and greasy. The pastry will also become difficult to work with if it becomes too warm. As with all pastries, care must be taken not to overwork it when mixing and rolling out or it may shrink and toughen during cooking. Always rest the finished pastry in the refrigerator before rolling it out and again when it is in the tin(s) before baking. This assists in preventing shrinkage and toughening of the pastry.

1 Rub in the butter using your fingertips, with your palms facing upwards so you can lift and aerate the flour mixture.

2 Use a flat-bladed knife to gradually incorporate the liquid ingredients into the dry ingredients until a coarse dough forms.

3 Knead the dough lightly, just a few times, until it is smooth.

4 Shape the dough into a disc and wrap in plastic wrap.

Shortcrust pastry

PREPARATION TIME 10 minutes (+ 30 minutes chilling)
MAKES enough to line a shallow 24 cm (9½ inch) fluted tart (flan) tin or four 8 cm (3¼ inch) fluted tart tins

260 g (9¼ oz/1¾ cups) plain (all-purpose) flour
½ teaspoon salt
125 g (4½ oz) chilled unsalted butter, diced
1 egg yolk
2 teaspoons lemon juice
1 tablespoon chilled water, approximately

1 Sift the flour and salt together into a large bowl. With your palms facing upwards, use your fingertips to rub in the butter, lifting the flour mixture up as you rub to aerate it, until the mixture resembles fine breadcrumbs (*pic 1*).

2 Make a well in the centre of the dry ingredients. Whisk together the egg yolk, lemon juice and water. Add to the dry ingredients and use a flat-bladed knife to gradually incorporate until a coarse dough forms, adding a little more water if necessary (*pic 2*).

3 Press the dough together — it should be soft, but not sticky. Turn it out onto a lightly floured, cool work surface and lightly knead just a few times, until the dough is smooth (*pic 3*).

4 Shape the dough into a disc and then wrap in plastic wrap (*pic 4*). Place in the refrigerator for 30 minutes to rest before rolling out and using as desired.

VARIATIONS
Parmesan shortcrust pastry: After rubbing in butter, add 35 g (1¼ oz/⅓ cup) finely grated parmesan cheese.

Herb shortcrust pastry: After rubbing in the butter, add 1 tablespoon finely chopped chives and 1 tablespoon finely chopped basil leaves.

Sweet shortcrust pastry

PREPARATION TIME 10 minutes (+ 30 minutes chilling)
MAKES enough to line a shallow 24 cm (9½ inch) fluted tart (flan) tin, four 8 cm (3¼ inch) fluted tart tins or 24 patty pan holes

225 g (8 oz/1½ cups) plain (all-purpose) flour
30 g (1 oz/¼ cup) icing (confectioners') sugar
½ teaspoon salt
125 g (4½ oz) chilled unsalted butter, cubed
1 egg, lightly whisked
Chilled water (optional)

1 Sift the flour, icing sugar and salt together into a large bowl. With your palms facing upwards, use your fingertips to rub in the butter, lifting the flour mixture up as you rub to aerate it, until the mixture resembles fine breadcrumbs (*pic 1*).

2 Make a well in the centre of the dry ingredients. Add the whisked egg and use a flat-bladed knife to gradually incorporate until a coarse dough forms, adding a little water if necessary (*pic 2*).

3 Press the dough together — it should be soft, but not sticky. Turn it out onto a lightly floured, cool work surface and lightly knead a few times, until the dough is smooth (*pic 3*).

4 Shape the dough into a disc and then wrap in plastic wrap (*pic 4*). Place in the refrigerator for 30 minutes to rest before rolling out and using as desired.

VARIATIONS
Almond shortcrust pastry: Replace 75 g (2¾ oz/½ cup) of the flour with 50 g (1¾ oz/½ cup) almond meal and reduce the butter to 100 g (3½ oz).

Brown sugar shortcrust pastry: Replace the icing sugar with 65 g (2¼ oz/⅓ cup, lightly packed) light brown sugar.

TIP Both shortcrust pastries can be made up to 3 days in advance and stored, wrapped in plastic wrap, in the refrigerator. Set aside at room temperature to soften slightly before rolling out. Uncooked pastry can be frozen, wrapped well in plastic wrap and then sealed in a freezer bag, for up to 4 weeks. Place it in the refrigerator to thaw completely, rather than leaving it out at room temperature.

Pâte brisée (rich shortcrust pastry)

In pastry making, the rich, crumbly texture and tenderness of good pastry is what is referred to as 'short'. Pâte brisée is an excellent, all-purpose rich pastry that is well suited to savoury tarts and pies as it contains no sugar. It is slightly richer than regular shortcrust pastry, which usually has a strict ratio of 1:2 for fat to flour. The ratio here is slightly higher. You can replace half the butter with lard if you like — lard gives pastry an even more flaky and tender quality than butter and has an incomparably rich flavour.

PREPARATION TIME 10 minutes (+ 30 minutes chilling)
MAKES enough to line a 26 cm (10½ inch) tart (flan) tin

250 g (9 oz/1⅔ cups) plain (all-purpose) flour
Pinch of salt
175 g (6 oz) chilled unsalted butter, chopped
60–80 ml (2–2½ fl oz/¼–⅓ cup) chilled water, approximately

1 Combine the flour and salt in a large bowl. Add the butter and use a pastry scraper or pastry cutter to cut the butter into the flour until the butter is the size of small peas. With your palms facing upwards, use your fingertips to rub in the butter, lifting the flour mixture up as you rub to aerate it, until the mixture resembles fine breadcrumbs.

2 Form the mixture into a mound, then make a well in the centre. Add 60 ml (2 fl oz/¼ cup) of the chilled water and use the fingertips of one hand to swirl the liquid in the well, bringing the flour mixture gradually in contact with the liquid until the liquid is evenly distributed. You will have a ragged heap of dough (*pic 1*).

3 Starting at the furthest side of the heap and working away from you, use the heel of your hand to smear the mixture forward (*pic 2*) in a quick, smooth, sliding action, continuing until all the mixture has been smeared and a dough starts to form. Add a little extra chilled water if a smooth dough doesn't begin to form. (The amount of water required will depend on how dry your flour is and how humid the air is.) You may need to repeat the smearing process two or three times until the mixture comes together smoothly.

4 Gather the dough together and press into a disc, about 2.5 cm (1 inch) thick (*pic 3*). Wrap in plastic wrap and refrigerate for 30 minutes to rest before rolling out and using as desired.

TIP For a richer pastry, reduce the chilled water to 1–2 tablespoons and add 1 chilled egg, whisked lightly with 1 chilled egg yolk, to the well. Add a little extra chilled water later, if needed.

1 After using your fingers to swirl the flour mixture gradually into the liquid you will have a ragged heap of dough.

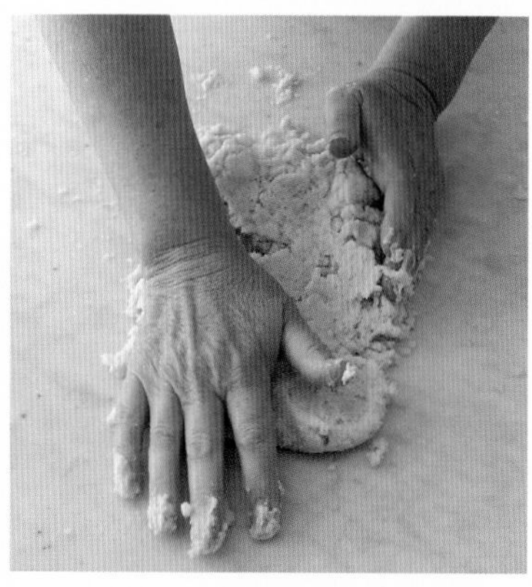

2 Use the heel of your hand to smear the mixture forwards in a quick, smooth, sliding action until a dough starts to form.

3 When the mixture comes together smoothly, gather it together and press into a disc, about 2.5 cm (1 inch) thick.

Pâte sucrée

Pâte sucrée has a wonderful biscuit-like flavour and texture, and is generally used for sweet tarts with fillings that don't require baking, such as fruit tarts. The dough is very fragile and easily over-handled, which makes it too soft to work with. If your pastry becomes too soft to roll, wrap it in plastic wrap and refrigerate for 15 minutes. Avoid using too much flour when rolling, as it can be absorbed into the pastry and make it heavy when cooked. Use a clean pastry brush to brush any excess flour from the dough.

PREPARATION TIME 10 minutes (+ 30–45 minutes chilling)
MAKES enough to line a 24 cm (9½ inch) fluted tart (flan) tin, four 8 cm (3¼ inch) tart tins or ten 6 cm (2½ inch) tart tins

250 g (9 oz/1⅔ cups) plain (all-purpose) flour
½ teaspoon salt
110 g (3¾ oz/½ cup) caster (superfine) sugar
150 g (5½ oz) unsalted butter, cut into 1.5 cm (⅝ inch) cubes and left at room temperature for 10 minutes
3 egg yolks, lightly whisked

1 Sift the flour and salt together into a large bowl. Stir in the sugar. With your palms facing upwards, use your fingertips to rub in the butter, lifting the flour mixture up as you rub to aerate it, until the mixture resembles fine breadcrumbs (*pic 1*).

2 Make a well in the centre of the dry ingredients. Add the egg yolks (*pic 2*) and use your fingertips to gradually incorporate until a coarse dough forms.

3 Turn the dough out onto a lightly floured, cool work surface. Quickly and lightly knead the dough (*pic 3*) to distribute the butter and eggs evenly, until it is smooth. Shape into a disc and wrap in plastic wrap. Refrigerate for 30–45 minutes to rest before rolling out and using as desired.

VARIATION

Chocolate pâte sucrée: Reduce the flour to 225 g (8 oz/1½ cups). Sift in 30 g (1 oz/¼ cup) unsweetened cocoa powder with the flour and salt.

TIP This pastry can be rolled and placed in a tin, then frozen. There's no need to thaw it before baking.
In hot weather, it helps if all the ingredients are chilled, even the flour.

1 With your palms facing upwards, use your fingertips to rub in the butter, lifting the flour mixture up as you rub to aerate it.

2 Make a well in the centre of the dry ingredients and add the egg yolks.

3 Turn the dough out onto a lightly floured, cool work surface. Quickly and lightly knead the dough until it is smooth.

Rolling out pastry

Before rolling pastry, it may help to let it stand at room temperature for 20–30 minutes or until slightly pliable, so it can be rolled easily. A cool work surface, such as a slab of marble, is preferable to prevent the pastry becoming too warm. The work surface and rolling pin should be lightly floured (not too much as the dough may incorporate it). Pastry is usually rolled to a thickness of 3–5 mm (1/8–1/4 inch).

1 Always roll from the centre of the pastry out to the edges and in the same direction. Turn the pastry regularly to ensure it is rolled evenly and doesn't stick to the work surface.

2 Carefully, and loosely, roll the pastry around the rolling pin and lift it over the tin, then carefully unroll it.

3 Use your fingers to carefully ease the pastry into the base and side of the tin, ensuring it's pressed into the base edge.

4 Roll the rolling pin over the top of the tin to trim the excess pastry.

Making small tarts (tartlets)

It is generally not necessary to grease tart (flan) tins as the pastry's butter content prevents it sticking. However, it is advisable to grease small tart tins, especially if they are deep, because pastry used for small tarts is usually rolled thinner than for larger tarts.

After the pastry is rolled and shapes are cut for tartlets, use your fingers to carefully transfer each piece to a tin. Ease the pastry into the tin, using your fingers to fit it snugly where the base meets the side (this will ensure the finished tart has a neat shape).

Trim the excess pastry by rolling the rolling pin over the top of each tin or by pressing on the edges with your fingers. Always refrigerate the pastry once it is in the tin, as this allows it to relax before baking and minimises the risk of shrinkage.

If you are rolling out small portions of pastry between two sheets of baking paper, lift the top layer of paper off and then carefully invert the pastry over the tart tin, using the other piece of paper to guide it into place. Remove the paper and proceed as above.

Blind baking

Some pastry shells need to be partially or completely cooked to make them crisp and prevent them becoming soggy once the filling is added. This is called 'blind baking'. Whether the pastry is partially or completely cooked depends on the filling. Moist fillings that will be baked in the pastry shell (such as baked custard-based fillings or frangipane) require the pastry to be partially cooked. Fillings that won't be baked (such as pastry cream) need to go into completely cooked, and cooled, pastry shells.

1 Place an octagon of baking paper (see tip) inside the chilled pastry shell to cover, pressing it gently into the edges of the tin.

2 Fill the pastry shell three-quarters full with baking beads, dried beans or uncooked rice, making sure they reach the sides.

3 Bake the pastry shell in the preheated oven, as directed, then lift out the paper and weights. Use the pastry as directed.

4 If cooking the shell completely, return it to the oven and cook as directed. Cool it completely on a wire rack before filling.

TIP To make a paper octagon, take a square of baking paper large enough to cover the base and side of the pastry shell generously. Fold it in half twice, so you end up with a small square. Fold the square in half diagonally to make a triangle, then again to make a thin triangle with a tail. Cut the tail off, then open it out — you should have an octagon about 5 cm (2 inches) larger than the diameter of the tin.

Making shortcrust pastry in the food processor

The food processor can make short work of shortcrust pastry (see pages 16–17), but you must be careful not to overwork the dough. Use the pulse button to process briefly until the dough just starts to cling together and is soft, but not sticky, then turn it out and knead lightly until smooth.

1 Process the flour, icing sugar (if using), salt and butter until the mixture resembles coarse breadcrumbs.

2 Add the wet ingredients, such as egg and/or water, and use the pulse button to process briefly until the dough just starts to cling together, adding a little extra water if necessary

Freezing raw and cooked pastry shells

To freeze uncooked pastry shells (whether shortcrust, sweet shortcrust, pâte brisée or pâte sucrée), simply wrap the pastry and tin in plastic wrap and freeze for up to 6 weeks. You can also freeze the rolled pastry (before it goes into the tin), wrapped well in plastic wrap and then sealed inside an airtight plastic bag, for up to 6 weeks.

It is important to wrap pastry well because any ice that forms on it will cause soft spots during baking. Pastry can be blind baked directly from frozen or it can be thawed slightly (not too much, as warming up isn't good for it).

Cooked pastry shells can also be frozen for up to 6 weeks. Again, it is vital that no ice be allowed to form on the surface or the thawed pastry will be ruined. Freezing is particularly useful for small tartlet cases, as you can pre-cook a large batch to have on hand as needed.

Using filo pastry

Filo pastry is wafer-thin and requires specialist knowledge and technical know-how to make by hand, so commercial filo is most suitable for home-baking. The sheets are very dry, so filo pastry is always baked in layers, with melted butter brushed generously between each. It is important to work with one sheet at a time and keep the remaining sheets covered with a damp tea towel (dish towel), as the pastry dries out quickly upon contact with air and becomes brittle. Filo is available both chilled and frozen, though the frozen variety is more fragile and can be difficult to work with.

1 Keep the sheets of filo in a neat stack covered with a damp tea towel, within easy reach.

2 Place one sheet on a work surface and brush all over with melted butter.

3 Place another sheet over the top to neatly cover, then brush that sheet with butter. Continue stacking and brushing the filo until you have the number of layers the recipe requires.

4 If the recipe requires you to cut the stack into smaller pieces, use a large, sharp knife.

Puff pastry

Mastering the art of puff pastry demands no more than practice and patience, but your efforts will be well rewarded. Most commercial varieties are made using margarine and other vegetable fats, and because these have a higher melting point than butter they make the pastry rise more spectacularly. However, the flavour of a home-made version using good-quality unsalted butter far outweighs this. Each time you roll the pastry before folding, it should be three times as long as it is wide. Try to keep the edges straight, using a palette knife to straighten them if necessary. The palette knife also comes in handy for loosening the pastry if it sticks to the work surface when rolled. This recipe gives 81 layers, while extremely fine puff pastry made by a skilled pâtissier can have up to 730 layers! Make sure you chill the pastry between folds, as instructed, to allow it to rest.

PREPARATION TIME 45 minutes (+ 1 hour 20 minutes chilling)
MAKES about 550 g (1 lb 4 oz)

225 g (8 oz/1½ cups) plain (all-purpose) flour, sifted
½ teaspoon salt
200 g (7 oz) unsalted butter, softened slightly
90 ml (3 fl oz) chilled water, approximately

1 Combine the flour and salt in a large bowl. Cut 25 g (1 oz) of the butter into small pieces and add to the bowl. With your palms facing upwards, use your fingertips to rub in the butter, lifting the flour mixture up as you rub to aerate it, until the mixture resembles fine breadcrumbs. Sprinkle over the water and mix with a flat-bladed knife, using a cutting action, until a coarse dough forms. Use your hands to lightly knead, adding a little extra chilled water if necessary, until a soft, but not sticky, dough forms.

2 Shape the dough into a rectangle, about 10 x 15 cm (4 x 6 inches), then wrap in plastic wrap and refrigerate for 20 minutes to rest and firm slightly.

3 Check that the remaining butter is the same pliable consistency as the dough — if it looks oily, it is too soft and needs chilling.

4 Turn the dough out onto a very lightly floured work surface and use a rolling pin to roll it out, always rolling away from you, to a 12 x 36 cm (4½ x 14¼ inch) rectangle *(pic 1)*. Use the rolling pin or your hands to shape the butter into a square, slightly less than half the size of the dough, and place over half the pastry *(pic 2)*, leaving a border of about 1 cm (½ inch). Fold the edges up and over the butter *(pic 3)*, then fold the uncovered pastry over the butter to fully enclose *(pic 4)*.

5 Use the rolling pin to gently tap the pastry widthways to form neat ridges *(pic 5)*. Without turning the pastry, roll it out, always rolling away from you, until it forms a neat rectangle, about 12 x 36 cm (4½ x 14¼ inches) *(pic 6)*. Take care to keep the sides and ends straight, using a palette knife to straighten them if necessary.

6 Fold the bottom third of the pastry over *(pic 7)*, then the top third over *(pic 8)* to form a parcel shape. Turn the pastry 90 degrees *(pic 9)*, then use the rolling pin to gently tap the pastry widthways to form neat ridges again. Roll the pastry out, always rolling away from you, until it forms a neat rectangle, about 12 x 36 cm (4½ x 14¼ inches). Repeat the folding process, but do not tap to create ridges. Wrap in plastic wrap and refrigerate for 20 minutes.

7 Repeat this process twice; rolling, then turning, then rolling and resting the dough in the refrigerator. This gives a total of 6 rolls and folds (note that encasing the butter in the dough initially does not count as a roll or fold). Refrigerate for 20 minutes before using.

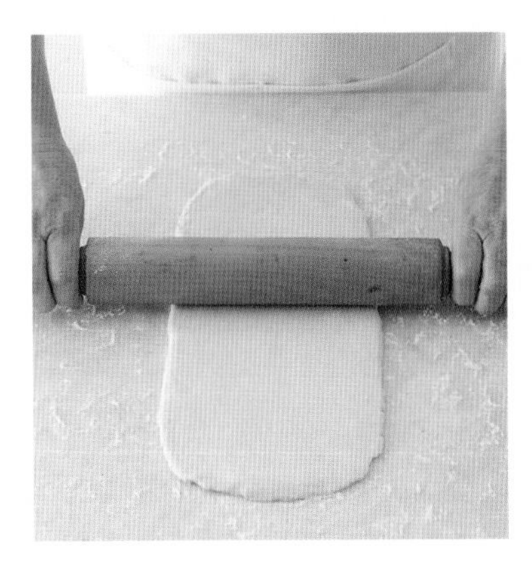

1 Use a rolling pin to roll out the dough to a long rectangle.

2 Place the butter over one half of the pastry, leaving a 1 cm (1/2 inch) border.

3 Fold the edges of the pastry up and over the butter.

4 Fold the uncovered pastry over the butter to fully enclose.

5 Use the rolling pin to gently tap the pastry widthways to form neat ridges.

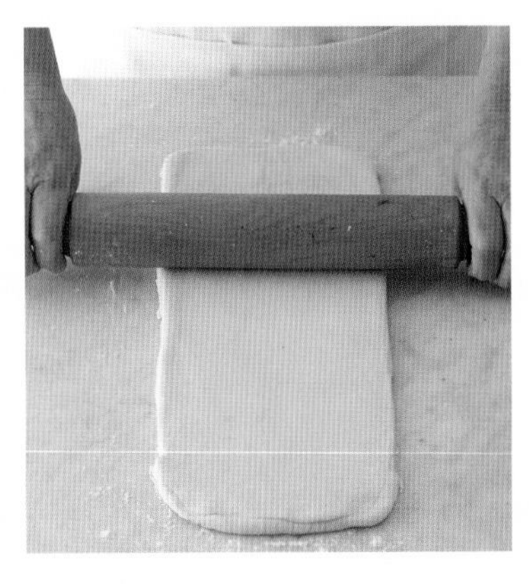

6 Roll the pastry out, rolling away from you, until it forms a neat rectangle.

7 Fold the bottom third of the pastry over.

8 Fold the top third of the pastry over to form a parcel shape.

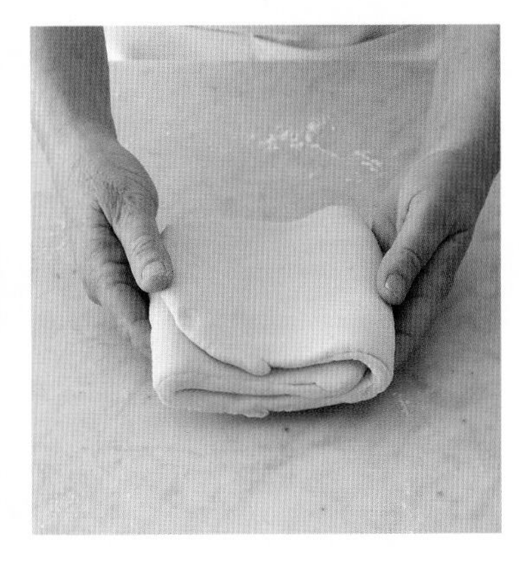

9 Turn the pastry 90 degrees.

Flaky pastry

Flaky pastry is like a less refined version of puff pastry. It is traditionally used in recipes where lift and delicacy are required but not to the degree that 'proper' puff would afford, such as in pasties, meat pies, sausage rolls, cream horns and fruit turnovers. Large lumps of butter are smeared over the detrempe (the name given to the initial dough mixture), then the butter is layered with the detrempe through a repeated sequence of rolling and turning. The detrempe needs to be rested well before the butter is incorporated or the finished pastry will be tough. It is also important not to stretch the detrempe or the pastry will shrink when baked. If the pastry starts to feel too soft while you are rolling it or the butter starts seeping out, place it in the refrigerator to allow the butter to firm slightly. Always rest the pastry when directed to ensure it remains tender and doesn't shrink when baked.

PREPARATION TIME 45 minutes (+ 1 hour 10 minutes chilling)
MAKES about 550 g (1 lb 4 oz)

225 g (8 oz/1½ cups) plain (all-purpose) flour, sifted
Pinch of salt
170 g (5¾ oz) chilled unsalted butter, chopped
90 ml (3 fl oz) chilled water, approximately

1 Combine the flour and salt in a large bowl. With your palms facing upwards, use your fingertips to rub in half the butter, lifting the flour mixture up as you rub to aerate it, until the mixture resembles fine breadcrumbs. Sprinkle over the chilled water and mix with a flat-bladed knife, using a cutting action, until a coarse dough forms. Use your hands to briefly knead, adding a little extra chilled water if necessary, until a firm and pliable, but not sticky, dough forms *(pic 1).*

2 Shape the pastry into a rectangle about 2 cm (¾ inch) thick, wrap in plastic wrap and refrigerate for 30 minutes to rest.

3 Turn the dough out onto a lightly floured work surface and use a rolling pin to roll out, always rolling away from you, to a rectangle, about 12 x 26 cm (4½ x 10½ inches) *(pic 2).* Dot half the remaining butter evenly over two-thirds of the pastry *(pic 3),* then use a palette knife to spread it out, leaving a 2 cm (¾ inch) border and one-third of the pastry uncovered. Fold over the unbuttered third of pastry *(pic 4).* Fold the remaining buttered pastry over the top *(pic 5)* to form a parcel shape *(pic 6).* Turn the pastry 90 degrees *(pic 7),* then gently press the edges with a rolling pin to seal *(pic 8).*

4 Roll the pastry out, always rolling away from you, until it forms a neat rectangle, about 12 x 36 cm (4½ x 14¼ inches). Repeat to fold, turn and seal the edges again. Wrap the pastry in plastic wrap and place in the refrigerator for 20 minutes to rest.

5 Roll the pastry out, always rolling away from you, until it forms a neat rectangle, about 12 x 36 cm (4½ x 14¼ inches). Dot the remaining butter over two-thirds of the pastry and smear as before. Repeat to fold, turn and seal the edges, then roll out again and fold, turn and seal once more. Wrap in plastic wrap and refrigerate for 20 minutes before using.

1 The dough should be firm and pliable, but not sticky.

2 Use a rolling pin to roll out the dough to a long rectangle.

3 Dot half the remaining butter evenly over two-thirds of the pastry.

4 Fold over the unbuttered third of pastry.

5 Fold the remaining buttered pastry over the top.

6 The pastry will form a neat parcel shape.

7 Turn the pastry 90 degrees.

8 Use a rolling pin to press the edges of the pastry to seal.

Rough puff pastry

Rough puff is basically a 'cheats' version of puff pastry. Large lumps of butter are tossed through the dough and the dough is then rolled and folded to intersperse the butter through the dough. This results in layers that are formed somewhat randomly and as a result the dough will rise to about twice its thickness when baked, which is much less than true puff pastry. It will also rise more unevenly than puff pastry. While not as elegant as puff pastry, rough puff is a great choice for pie toppings or pastries such as sausage rolls. It is a good substitute when you don't have the time required to make puff pastry.

PREPARATION TIME 45 minutes (+ 1 hour chilling)
MAKES about 550 g (1 lb 4 oz)

250 g (9 oz/1⅔ cups) plain (all-purpose) flour, sifted
Pinch of salt
150 g (5½ oz) unsalted butter, cut into 1 cm (½ inch) pieces, softened slightly
100 ml (3½ fl oz) chilled water, approximately

1 Combine the flour and salt in a large bowl. Add the butter and toss to coat in the flour. Sprinkle over the water and mix with a flat-bladed knife, using a cutting action, until a coarse dough forms *(pic 1)*. Use your hands to lightly knead, adding a little extra water if necessary, until a soft, but not sticky, dough forms *(pic 2)*.

2 Shape the dough into a rectangle, about 10 x 15 cm (4 x 6 inches) and 2 cm (¾ inch) thick *(pic 3)*. Wrap in plastic wrap and refrigerate for about 20 minutes. Do not chill the pastry for too long, as it will make the butter too hard and the pastry will tear when rolled and folded.

3 Turn the dough out onto a very lightly floured work surface and use a rolling pin to roll out the dough, always rolling away from you, to a 12 x 36 cm (4½ x 14¼ inch) rectangle *(pic 4)*. Use the rolling pin to gently tap the pastry widthways to form neat ridges *(pic 5)*. Use a palette knife to straighten the edges if necessary *(pic 6)*.

4 Fold the bottom third of the pastry over *(pic 7)*, then the top third over *(pic 8)* to form a parcel shape. Turn the pastry 90 degrees *(pic 9)*, then use the rolling pin to gently tap the pastry widthways to form neat ridges again. Roll the pastry out, always rolling away from you, until it forms a neat rectangle, about 12 x 36 cm (4½ x 14¼ inches). Repeat the folding process, but do not tap to create ridges. Wrap in plastic wrap and refrigerate for 20 minutes.

5 Repeat this process once more; rolling, folding and turning, then rolling, folding and resting the dough in the refrigerator. This gives a total of 4 rolls and folds. Refrigerate for 20 minutes before using.

1 Using a cutting action, mix with a flat-bladed knife until a coarse dough forms.

2 Use your hands to gently knead until a soft, but not sticky, dough forms.

3 Shape the dough into a rectangle, about 10 x 15 cm (4 x 6 inches).

4 Roll out the dough, rolling away from you, to 12 x 36 cm (4½ x 14¼ inches).

5 Use the rolling pin to gently tap the pastry widthways to make neat ridges.

6 Straighten the edges with a palette knife if necessary.

7 Fold the bottom third of the pastry over.

8 Fold the top third of the pastry over to form a parcel shape.

9 Turn the pastry 90 degrees.

Leavened puff pastry

Mastering this pastry is immensely satisfying, because the results are so exceptional. It's really no more challenging to make than puff pastry — the technique of rolling and turning the dough to layer the butter and detrempe is exactly the same, only this dough is leavened with yeast and therefore includes rising time. It results in a crisp, buttery, flaky pastry you'll recognise as that which is used for croissants. The croissant, whose name translates as 'crescent', is associated with France but it actually originated in Austria and was introduced to France in the 19th century. It became immensely popular there, and in the 1970s the rest of the world caught on to its charms thanks to the advent of industrial manufacturing methods. However, as with many foods, croissants that are made by hand are far superior.

PREPARATION TIME 55 minutes (+ 2½–3 hours proving and 1½ hours chilling)
MAKES 800 g (1 lb 12 oz), enough to make 10 croissants (see page 138)

60 ml (2 fl oz/¼ cup) warm water
9 g (¼ oz/2½ teaspoons) dried yeast
250 ml (9 fl oz/1 cup) warm milk
1 teaspoon sugar
500 g (1 lb 2 oz/3⅓ cups) plain (all-purpose) flour
1 teaspoon salt
310 g (11 oz) unsalted butter, softened slightly so it is firm but pliable

1 Put the warm water in a small bowl. Sprinkle over the yeast, then set aside for 6–7 minutes or until foamy. Mix in the milk and sugar.

2 Combine the flour and salt in a large bowl. With your palms facing upwards, use your fingertips to rub in 60 g (2¼ oz) of the butter, lifting to aerate the flour mixture as you rub until the mixture resembles fine breadcrumbs. Make a well in the centre, add the milk mixture and stir, gradually incorporating the dry ingredients, until a soft, sticky dough forms.

3 Turn the dough out onto a lightly floured work surface and knead for 5 minutes or until smooth and elastic. Place in a lightly oiled bowl, turning to coat in the oil. Cover the bowl with plastic wrap and set aside in a warm, draught-free place for 1½–2 hours or until doubled in size *(pic 1)*.

4 Knock back the dough with just one punch to expel the air. Cover the bowl again and set aside in a warm, draught-free place for another hour to rise. Knock back the dough once more *(pic 2)*. Shape the dough into a thick rectangle *(pic 3)*, wrap in plastic wrap and refrigerate for 30 minutes to chill.

5 Turn the dough out onto a cool, lightly floured surface and use a rolling pin to roll out, always rolling away from you, to a 16 x 32 cm (6¼ x 12¾ inch) rectangle, about 8 mm (⅜ inch) thick *(pic 4)*. Take care to keep the sides and ends straight, using a palette knife to straighten them if necessary. Dot the remaining butter evenly over two-thirds of the pastry, then use the palette knife to spread it out *(pic 5)*, leaving a 2 cm (¾ inch) border and one-third of the pastry uncovered.

6 Fold over the unbuttered third of pastry *(pic 6)*. Fold the remaining buttered pastry over the top *(pic 7)* to form a parcel shape. Use your fingers to press the edges to seal *(pic 8)*. Turn the pastry 90 degrees *(pic 9)*. Carefully roll the pastry out on a lightly floured work surface, always rolling away from you, until it forms a neat rectangle, about 16 x 32 cm (6¼ x 12¾ inches). Repeat the folding to make a parcel shape again. Wrap in plastic wrap and refrigerate for 30 minutes.

7 Repeat this process once more: place the pastry on a lightly floured surface, with the folded edge on your left, and roll, fold and turn, then roll and fold again. This gives a total of 4 rolls and folds. Wrap the dough in plastic wrap and refrigerate for 30 minutes or until firm before using.

1 Set the dough aside until it has doubled in size.

2 Knock back the dough.

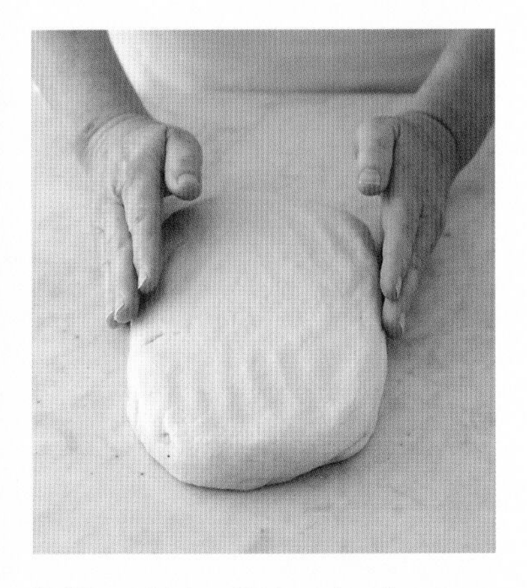

3 Shape it into a thick rectangle.

4 Roll the dough out to a 16 x 32 cm (6¼ x 12¾ inch) rectangle.

5 Spread the remaining butter over two-thirds of the pastry.

6 Fold over the unbuttered third of the pastry.

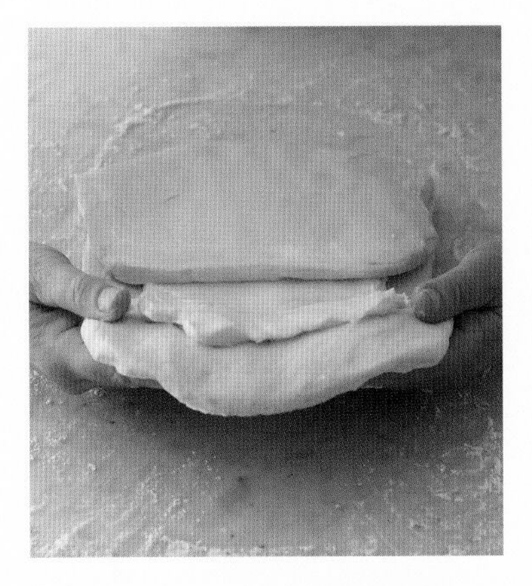

7 Fold the remaining buttered pastry over the top to form a parcel shape.

8 Press the edges to seal.

9 Turn the pastry 90 degrees.

Choux pastry

Choux pastry (pâte à choux) consists of a cooked dough, which makes it unique in the pastry world. It is believed that a 16th-century chef working for Catherine de Medici, the Italian-born French queen, created it and then the celebrated pastry chef Antonin Carême used it to make the éclair and croquembouche some 200 years later. Choux pastry contains no leavener, but rises by the action of the steam that forms when it is in the oven. While it is not difficult to make, the pastry's success depends on a few crucial elements: the flour and butter must be weighed accurately; the egg needs to be added gradually because the amount needed will vary according to the strength of your flour and the rate at which it absorbs liquid; and the oven door must not be opened (no peeping!) or it will not rise properly. Choux pastry is used for éclairs, profiteroles, gougères, paris brest, beignets and fritters.

PREPARATION TIME 20 minutes
cooking time 7 minutes
MAKES enough for 12 éclairs or about 30 profiteroles

1/2 teaspoon salt
1 1/2 teaspoons caster (superfine) sugar
125 g (4 1/2 oz) plain (all-purpose) flour, sifted
60 g (2 1/4 oz) unsalted butter, chopped, at room temperature
3–4 large eggs, lightly whisked

1 Combine the salt, sugar and flour in a bowl and set aside. Put 150 ml (5 fl oz) water and the butter in a medium saucepan and bring slowly to the boil; the butter should melt before it comes to the boil *(pic 1)*.

2 Working quickly, remove the saucepan from the heat, add the flour mixture all at once and stir vigorously with a wooden spoon to combine *(pic 2)*. Return the saucepan to low heat and cook, stirring vigorously, for about 1 minute or until the mixture forms a smooth, thick mass that comes away from the side of the pan *(pic 3)*. Do not overbeat the mixture or the pastry will not rise properly.

3 Transfer the mixture to the bowl of a stand mixer fitted with the paddle attachment and set aside for 5 minutes or until cooled slightly. Gradually add the egg, beating constantly and ensuring it's mixed in well before adding more *(pic 4)*. Continue beating in the egg until the mixture is glossy and falls heavily from the beaters *(pic 5)*. The mixture should fold in on itself when cut through with a spatula *(pic 6)*. You may not need all of the egg.

4 The pastry can be baked immediately, as directed in the specific recipe, or covered tightly and refrigerated for up to 24 hours. Bring to room temperature before using.

TIP To make choux pastry by hand, allow it to cool until warm in the saucepan, then use a wooden spoon to beat constantly while gradually adding the egg, ensuring it's mixed in before adding more. Continue beating in the egg until the mixture is glossy and falls heavily from the spoon.

If making a double quantity of choux pastry, you will need to cool the mixture for longer before adding the egg, as the larger quantity means it will hold the heat well and you don't want the egg to cook. Set it aside for up to 10 minutes and then beat for 2–3 minutes once the egg is added.

1 The butter should melt before the mixture comes to the boil.

2 Add the flour mixture all at once and stir vigorously with a wooden spoon to combine.

3 Cook, stirring vigorously, until the mixture forms a smooth, thick mass that comes away from the side of the pan.

4 Gradually add the egg, beating constantly and ensuring it's mixed in before adding more.

5 Continue beating in the egg until the mixture is glossy and falls heavily from the beaters.

6 The mixture should fold in on itself when cut with a spatula.

Piping/shaping choux pastry

Choux pastry is easy to deal with as, unlike conventional pastries, if you have made it to the correct consistency it won't shrink or toughen in the oven. It does help to use a piping (icing) bag for many choux-based recipes as this will provide the neatest and most consistent shapes. Due to the heat and consistency of the mixture, you will need a good-sized strong bag, available from kitchenware stores.

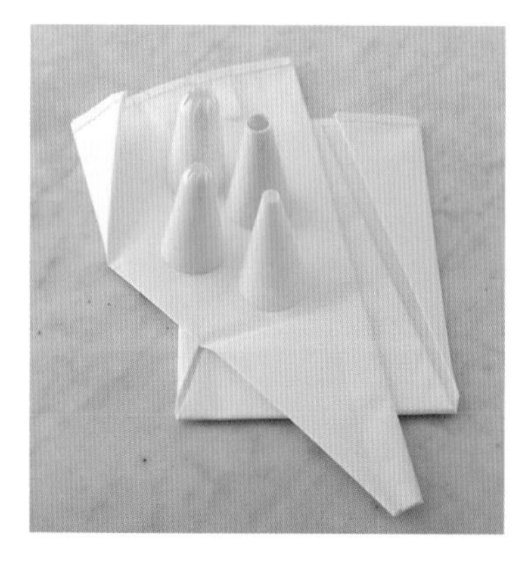

1 Nozzles are usually made of plastic and are either plain or fluted. They also come in various sizes.

2 Place the nozzle in the bag, then fold the bag back over one hand to open it out.

3 Spoon enough choux pastry into the bag to fill it about halfway, taking care not to overfill.

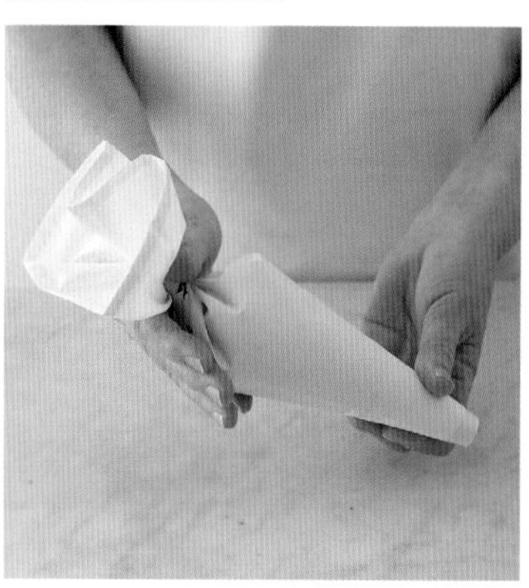

4 Twist the bag lightly so it feels tight and the pastry is firmly contained. Use the hand you write with to firmly grip the bag where it is twisted and use your other hand to gently hold the nozzle to guide it.

5 Hold the bag firmly and on a slightly diagonal angle, with the nozzle nearly touching the lined tray. Apply gentle pressure with the hand that is gripping the bag to push the pastry out through the nozzle, moving the bag smoothly at the same time to create a line (for éclairs or paris brest). For profiteroles, hold the nozzle directly over the tray and pipe small rounds.

6 When you have finished piping the shape, pipe back a little onto the pastry to avoid a peaked end. If you do end up with ends that stick out, push them down gently with a damp finger. If you need a particular size or shape of pastry, mark it on the baking paper in pencil and then turn the paper over before piping. Allow about 1 cm (1/2 inch) for spreading. For more rustic pastries, scoop up some pastry with a spoon and scrape it off into a neat pile using another spoon.

Crème pâtissière (pastry cream)

Pastry cream is one of the fundamental preparations of the classic French culinary repertoire. It is simple to make and is used as a filling for baked goods such as éclairs, profiteroles and fruit tarts. The most common fault is lumpiness — to prevent this it is important to constantly stir, or whisk, the thickening custard over the heat. Unlike other types of custard, pastry cream must boil or it will not thicken properly and the flour will not cook. Place a cartouche on the surface once it is cooked to avoid a thick skin forming. Vanilla is the most common flavouring for this custard and you will get the best results by using seeds scraped from a split vanilla bean. Although it is more expensive than vanilla extracts and other vanilla products, the flavour of real vanilla is incomparable.

PREPARATION TIME 25 minutes
MAKES 660 g (1 lb 7 oz/2 2/3 cups)

1 vanilla bean, split lengthways and seeds scraped
250 ml (9 fl oz/1 cup) milk
250 ml (9 fl oz/1 cup) pouring (whipping) cream
4 egg yolks
150 g (5 1/2 oz/2/3 cup) caster (superfine) sugar
2 tablespoons plain (all-purpose) flour
1 tablespoon cornflour (cornstarch)

1 Put the vanilla seeds, milk and cream in a medium heavy-based saucepan over medium heat and bring just to a simmer. Remove from the heat.

2 Use an electric mixer to whisk the egg yolks and sugar in a mixing bowl until thick and pale *(pic 1)*. Sift together the flour and cornflour, then use a balloon whisk to whisk into the yolk mixture until smooth and well combined. Pour about half the hot milk mixture onto the yolk mixture and whisk until smooth, then whisk in the remaining milk. Clean the pan. Return the mixture to the cleaned pan.

3 Stirring constantly with the balloon whisk to prevent lumps, bring the mixture slowly to the boil over medium heat. Reduce the heat and simmer, whisking often, for 2 minutes, until thick and smooth *(pic 2)*.

4 Remove from the heat. Transfer to a glass or metal bowl and place a cartouche (a round of non-stick baking paper) on the surface to prevent a skin forming *(pic 3)*. Cool to room temperature. Whisk with a balloon whisk until smooth before using. Crème pâtissière can be refrigerated in an airtight container for up to 2 days.

1 Whisk the egg yolks and sugar until thick and pale.

2 Reduce the heat and simmer, whisking often, for 2 minutes, until thick and smooth.

3 Place a cartouche on the surface to prevent a skin forming.

Pastry definitions

Baking blind The pre-baking (either completely or partially) of a pastry shell. The pastry is placed in the tin, then covered with baking paper and filled with baking beads, dried beans or uncooked rice to provide weight before being pre-baked. This prevents the pastry from puffing up at the base or slumping at the side.

Cartouche A round of baking paper that is placed directly on the surface of crème pâtissière, custard and similar mixtures, to prevent a skin forming. A cartouche is cut to cover the surface area exactly, so it is particularly effective. A piece of plastic wrap can also be used.

Crimp A technique that seals the edges of pastry and also creates a decorative finish. It can be done using the tines of a fork or your fingertips (each recipe will specify which to use).

Detrempe When making laminated pastries (flaky, puff, rough puff, and so on), flour, water and a small amount of fat are initially mixed to form a firm dough, called the detrempe. Egg wash A mixture of egg or egg yolk and a small quantity of water or milk that is whisked until smooth and brushed over raw pastry or bread dough to give a shine once cooked.

Glaze Applying a liquid to buns or pastries to create a shiny surface. Glazes can be applied before cooking — a mixture of egg yolk and milk (egg wash) is commonly used or it can be beaten egg white or just milk — or after baking, such as sieved, warm apricot jam or a thick sugar syrup.

Greasing This prevents a baked item sticking to the tin or baking tray during cooking. Oil or soft or melted butter can be used and should be applied very thinly to the tin or tray. Sometimes tins are lightly dusted with flour after greasing.

Laminated pastries This term includes pastries whose delicate, airy qualities are achieved by the careful layering of butter and dough, such as puff and flaky pastries. When they are baked, the liquid in the butter converts to steam, which creates lift. The process of rolling and folding the layers of butter into the dough is called 'laminating'.

Piping Forming neat lines or shapes of a mixture using a special piping (icing) bag fitted with a nozzle/tip. Icings (frostings), choux pastry (see page 44) and the decorative crosses on hot cross buns all require piping.

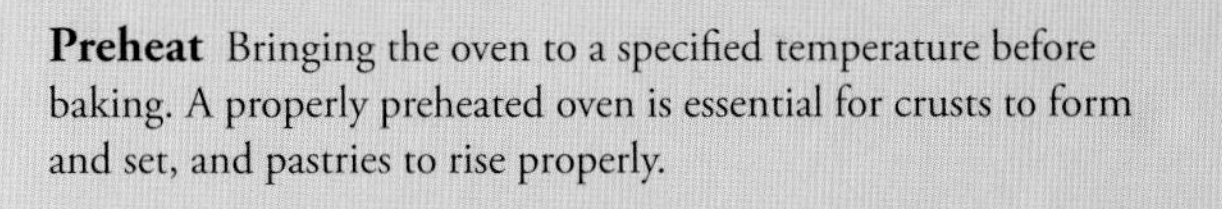

Preheat Bringing the oven to a specified temperature before baking. A properly preheated oven is essential for crusts to form and set, and pastries to rise properly.

Resting After handling pastry, it is necessary to let it sit for a while, generally in the refrigerator. This 'resting' time allows any gluten that may have formed to relax. Gluten can develop when water is added to a dough, after rolling out dough or when dough is handled too much.

Rubbing in Using your fingertips to incorporate butter into dry ingredients. When it has been rubbed in successfully the mixture will resemble breadcrumbs (each recipe will specify fine or coarse breadcrumbs).

Pie and Tart decorations

A simple decoration on pastry somehow makes a pie or tart seem more appealing, so take the opportunity to make full use of your creative skills. Traditionally, savoury pies were decorated to differentiate them from sweet pies when both were served at a meal. These days, we use trimmings mainly for decorative effect. Pies are usually double-crusted (a pastry base and top) or with just a lid on top, whereas tarts are generally open with no pastry top. As well as giving pies a finished touch, decorating can be very practical. Not only can you use up pastry trimmings but it helps seal the edges of a double-crusted pie so the lid remains securely in place.

Decorative edges

Fork-pressed To achieve this effect, simply press a lightly floured fork around the crust's edge.

Fluted Press the pastry between your thumb and forefinger for a rippled effect.

Crimped Press the pastry between the thumb and forefinger, while indenting with the other forefinger.

Scalloped Press an upturned teaspoon on the pastry edges to mark semi-circles.

Checkerboard Make cuts in the pastry edge. Bend every second square inward.

Leaves Cut out leaf shapes with a cutter or the point of a sharp knife and mark veins using the back of a knife. Attach to the lip of the pie using a little water or egg glaze.

Plait Cut three long strips 5 mm (¼ inch) wide. Plait together and attach to the lip of the pie using a little water or egg glaze, pressing gently in place.

Rope Twist two long sausages of pastry together and attach to the edge with a little water or egg glaze.

Feathering Lift the pastry off the lip so that it stands upright and snip diagonally into the edge of the pie. Push one point inwards and one point outwards.

Decorative tops

There are endless shapes and forms you can use to decorate pies, from cherries and stars to abstract patterns, or simple initials. Alternatively, you can buy small biscuit cutters in various shapes. When rolling out the pastry trimmings, don't make the shapes too thick or they won't cook through. To attach them, first brush the pie lid with an egg glaze, then arrange the decorations and glaze them as well.

You can decorate an open tart with pastry shapes, either around the edge or on top. However, if the filling is quite liquid, cook the shapes separately and arrange on the tart after it is baked and the filling has set.

Another impressive finish for a pie is a lattice top, which is shown on some of the sweet pies in this book. However, it is equally suitable for savoury pies and is surprisingly simple to make. Roll the pastry out on a sheet of baking paper to a square a little larger than the pie. Using a fluted pastry wheel or a small sharp knife, cut strips of pastry about 1.5 cm (⅝ inch) wide. On another sheet of baking paper, lay half the strips vertically, 1 cm (½ inch) apart. Fold back alternate strips of pastry and lay a strip of pastry horizontally across the unfolded strips, then fold the vertical strips back into place. Next, fold the lower strips back and lay another piece horizontally. Repeat with all the strips. Refrigerate until firm, then invert the lattice onto the pie and remove the baking paper. Press the edges to seal and trim the excess pastry.

You can vary the width of the strips and also the spacing, to create a tightly woven lattice or one with just a few strips. Alternatively, you can make life very simple and buy a lattice cutter. Just roll it over the pastry, then gently open it out, lift it onto your pie and trim the edges, as before.

Large Pies & Tarts

Quiche lorraine

Quiche is an open tart with an egg-based filling that originated in Lorraine, France. Bacon, eggs and cheese feature in the traditional quiche lorraine filling, though it's easy to vary the flavours once you have mastered the classic recipe. Try our variations, then create your own flavour combinations.

SERVES 4–6 **PREPARATION TIME** 30 minutes (+ 45 minutes chilling) **COOKING TIME** 1 hour

1 quantity shortcrust pastry (see pages 16-17)
2 teaspoons olive oil
1 brown onion, finely chopped
4 bacon rashers (slices), rind removed, finely chopped
50 g (1¾ oz/½ cup, loosely packed) coarsely grated gruyère cheese
¼ cup snipped chives
3 eggs
250 ml (9 fl oz/1 cup) pouring (whipping) cream
125 ml (4 fl oz/½ cup) milk

1 Roll the pastry out between 2 sheets of non-stick baking paper to a disc 4 mm (¼ inch) thick. Roll the pastry around the rolling pin and carefully ease it into a 3.5 cm (1½ inch) deep, 24 cm (9½ inch) fluted, loose-based tart (flan) tin, pressing it into the edges with your fingertips (see page 28). Trim any excess pastry by rolling the rolling pin over the top of the tin. Cover with plastic wrap and place in the refrigerator for 15 minutes to rest.

2 Preheat the oven to 200°C (400°F/Gas 6). Place the tart tin on a baking tray. Line the pastry shell with non-stick baking paper, then fill with baking beads, dried beans or rice. Bake for 10 minutes, then remove the beads and paper. Bake for a further 10 minutes or until the pastry is light golden-brown and just cooked through.

3 Meanwhile, heat the oil in a frying pan over medium heat. Add the onion and bacon and cook, stirring, for 3–5 minutes or until the bacon is crisp. Transfer onto paper towels to drain and set aside to cool *(pic 1)*.

4 Reduce the oven temperature to 180°C (350°F/Gas 4). Sprinkle the bacon mixture, cheese and chives over the cooked pastry shell *(pic 2)*. Whisk the eggs in a medium jug, then whisk in the cream and milk. Pour into the pastry shell *(pic 3)*. Bake for 35–40 minutes or until the filling has just set. Remove from oven and leave in tin for 5 minutes before removing. Serve warm or at room temperature.

VARIATIONS

Pancetta and zucchini quiche: Use 1 quantity herb shortcrust pastry (see page 17). Replace the bacon with 150 g (5½ oz) pancetta slices, thinly sliced. Cook 2 small zucchini, thinly sliced, with the pancetta and onion, and cook for 6–8 minutes. Replace the gruyère with cheddar cheese and the chives with chopped basil.

Spinach and feta quiche: Use 1 quantity parmesan shortcrust pastry (see page 17). Omit the bacon. Add 150 g (5½ oz) baby spinach leaves and 1 tablespoon lemon juice to the cooked onion, and cook for a further 1–2 minutes or until the spinach wilts. Replace the gruyère with 100 g (3½ oz) crumbled feta and 50 g (1¾ oz/½ cup) finely grated parmesan.

1

2

3

TIP Keep in an airtight container in the refrigerator for up to 2 days.

Silverbeet pie

This pie is similar to spanakopita, the famous spinach and feta pie so common throughout Greece. You don't need to make the pastry yourself so it is quick and easy to put together, perfect for a picnic.

SERVES 8 **PREPARATION TIME** 20 minutes **COOKING TIME** 1½ hours

1 tablespoon olive oil
2 spring onions (scallions), thinly sliced
1 bunch (about 545 g/1 lb 3½ oz) silverbeet (Swiss chard), trimmed and thinly sliced
2 tablespoons finely chopped dill
1 tablespoon finely chopped mint
2 teaspoons finely grated lemon zest
310 g (11 oz/1⅓ cups) firm, fresh ricotta cheese
4 eggs, lightly whisked
200 g (7 oz/1½ cups) crumbled feta cheese
10 sheets filo pastry
100 g (3½ oz) butter, melted
Lemon wedges, to serve

1 Heat the oil in a large frying pan over medium heat. Add the spring onions and cook, stirring occasionally, for 5 minutes. Add the silverbeet, cover and cook for 3 minutes or until wilted. Transfer to a colander to drain and cool completely. Use your hands to squeeze the mixture in the colander to remove as much liquid as possible.

2 Combine the dill, mint, zest, ricotta and egg in a bowl. Add the spinach mixture and feta, and season with salt and freshly ground black pepper. Stir until well combined.

3 Preheat the oven to 180°C (350°F/Gas 4). Lay one sheet of filo on a clean work surface, keeping the remaining sheets covered with a damp tea towel (dish towel) to prevent them drying out. Brush with some of the melted butter, then lay another sheet of filo on top. Repeat with the remaining sheets to make two stacks, each with 5 sheets of filo. Cut each stack widthways to make six 13 cm (5 inch) wide rectangles *(pic 1)*.

4 Grease the base and side of a round 22 cm (8½ inch) diameter spring-form cake tin. Place the filo rectangles over the base and side of the tin to line it fully, allowing the filo to overhang the side of the tin *(pic 2)*.

5 Spoon the spinach mixture into the filo-lined tin. Fold the overhanging filo over to enclose the filling *(pic 3)*. Brush with the remaining melted butter. Bake for 1 hour 20 minutes or until cooked through. Cool in the tin for at least 10 minutes before removing. Serve the pie warm or at room temperature with lemon wedges.

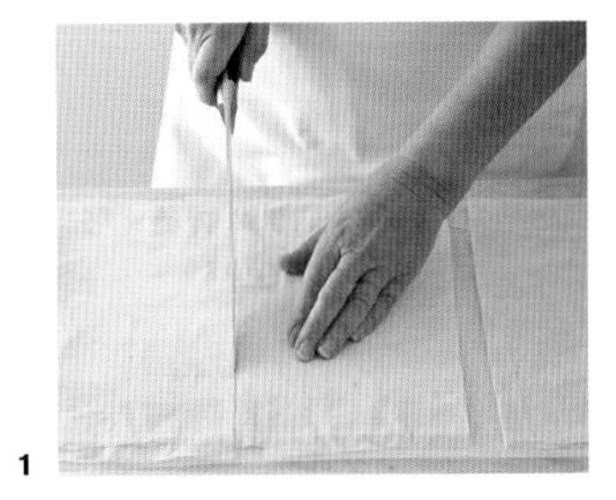

1

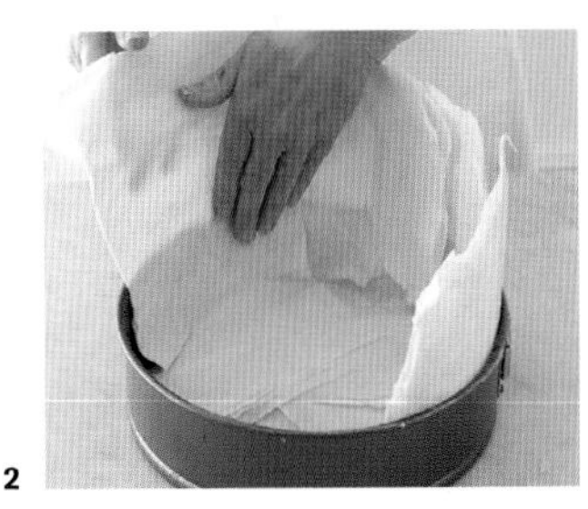

2

3

TIP This pie is best eaten on the day it is baked.

Pissaladière

SERVES 4–6 **PREPARATION TIME** 30 minutes (+ 30 minutes cooling) **COOKING TIME** 40–45 minutes

60 ml (2 fl oz/¼ cup) olive oil
1 kg (2 lb 4 oz) brown onions, halved and thinly sliced
½ teaspoon salt
4 sheets (25 x 25 cm/10 x 10 inches) frozen ready-rolled puff pastry, thawed
1 egg, lightly whisked
20–30 anchovies, halved lengthways
95 g (3¼ oz/½ cup) kalamata olives, pitted and halved
10 thyme sprigs

1 Heat a large heavy-based frying pan over medium–low heat. Add the oil, onions and salt and cook, stirring often, for 20–25 minutes or until the onions are soft and caramelised *(pic 1)*. Transfer to a bowl and set aside for 30 minutes or until cooled to room temperature.

2 Preheat the oven to 220°C (425°F/Gas 7). Line 2 baking trays with non-stick baking paper.

3 Place a pastry sheet on each lined tray. Brush lightly with the whisked egg (*pic 2*) and then place another sheet of pastry on top of each.

4 Use a very sharp knife to mark a 1 cm (½ inch) border around each pastry square, cutting only through the top sheet of pastry *(pic 3)*.

5 Divide the cooled onion mixture between the pastry squares and spread it out in an even layer to the border of each. Arrange the anchovies on top in a lattice pattern. Dot with the olive halves. Strip the leaves from the thyme sprigs and scatter over the top. Lightly brush the pastry border with a little of the remaining whisked egg.

6 Bake the pissaladière for 20 minutes or until the pastry is puffed and golden. Serve warm or at room temperature.

1

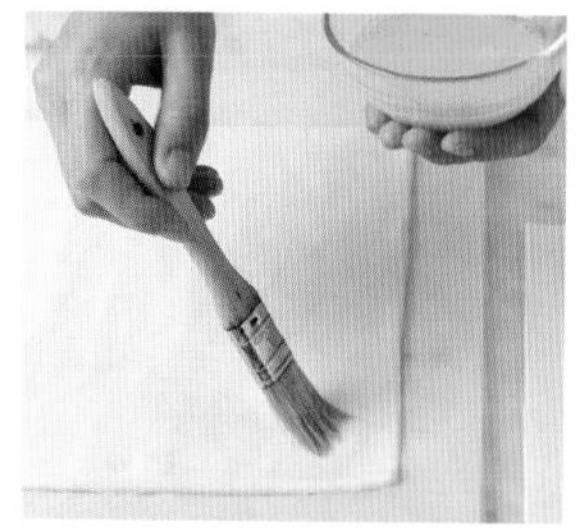
2

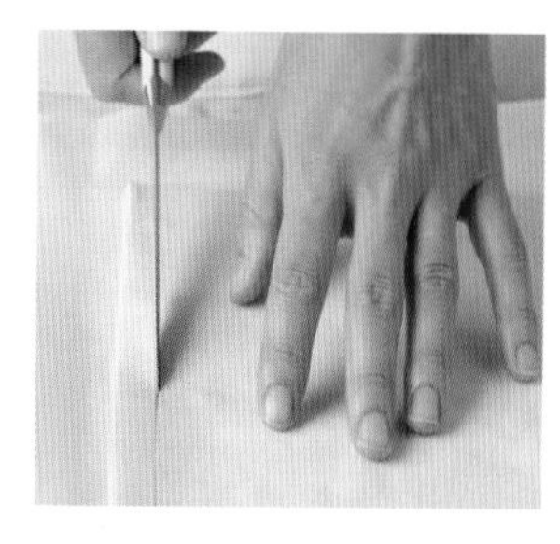
3

TIP You can also use a 375 g (13 oz) block of ready-made puff pastry. Use a lightly floured rolling pin to roll it out on a lightly floured work surface to 25 x 40 cm (10 x 16 inches) and about 4 mm (¼ inch) thick. Cut it in half and place on the lined trays. Refrigerate for 15 minutes or until firm. Do not brush with egg. When marking the border, cut only halfway into the pastry.

Roast onion tart

Perfect for a lunch party or light dinner, this tart needs no more than a simple green salad as an accompaniment. Roasting the onions makes them wonderfully sweet and smooth.

MAKES 26 cm (10½ inch) tart **PREPARATION TIME** 55 minutes (+ 1 hour chilling)
COOKING TIME 1 hour 35–40 minutes

1 quantity pâte brisée (see page 18)
700 g (1 lb 9 oz) brown onions (about 6)
90 ml (3 fl oz) olive oil
1¼ tablespoons balsamic vinegar
1 tablespoon caster (superfine) sugar
2 eggs
1 egg yolk
225 ml (7¾ fl oz) pouring (whipping) cream
225 ml (7¾ fl oz) milk
100 g (3½ oz/1 cup) finely grated parmesan cheese
2½ teaspoons thyme leaves, plus thyme sprigs, to garnish

1 Use a rolling pin to roll out the pastry on a lightly floured work surface to a circle, about 36 cm (14¼ inches) in diameter. Gently ease the pastry into a 2.5 cm (1 inch) deep, round 26 cm (10½ inch) fluted loose-based tart (flan) tin (see page 20). Roll the rolling pin over the tin to trim the excess pastry, then refrigerate for 30 minutes.

2 Preheat the oven to 180°C (350°F/Gas 4). Line the pastry shell with non-stick baking paper and fill with baking beads, dried beans or uncooked rice. Bake for 25 minutes, then remove from the oven. Remove the paper and weights and set the pastry shell aside.

3 Peel the onions, leaving the root ends intact. Cut in half, then cut each half into thirds lengthways and place in a single layer on a baking tray. Drizzle the olive oil, then the vinegar, over the onions and sprinkle with the sugar. Roast for 35 minutes, turning occasionally, or until deep golden and soft *(pic 1)*.

4 Meanwhile, whisk the eggs and egg yolk together in a medium bowl. Whisk in the cream and milk. Season with sea salt and freshly ground black pepper.

5 Scatter the parmesan over the pastry shell, then arrange the onions on top in concentric circles *(pic 2)*. Place the tin on a baking tray, then carefully pour the cream mixture over the onions *(pic 3)*. Scatter over the thyme leaves, then bake for 35–40 minutes or until the filling is just set. Remove from the oven and allow to cool slightly. Serve the tart warm or at room temperature, garnished with the thyme sprigs.

1

2

3

TIP You can vary the cheese and herbs if you like. Try cheddar and snipped chives, blue cheese and chopped sage, or gruyère and finely chopped rosemary.

Steak and kidney pie

This is a traditional British pie. Sometimes oysters, boiled eggs and potatoes are added. The cooled mixture is placed in a casserole dish and topped with a pastry crust. If the pie dish is deep, a decorative funnel, often in the shape of a bird, is placed in the centre of the pie to support the pastry and act as a steam vent during the long cooking. Another traditional dish, known as steak and kidney pudding, uses the same ingredients but they are placed, uncooked, in a pudding basin that is lined with suet pastry. The pudding is then steamed or baked.

SERVES 6 **PREPARATION TIME** 20 minutes **COOKING TIME** 1 hour 50 minutes

4 lamb kidneys
2 tablespoons plain (all-purpose) flour
750 g (1 lb 10 oz) round steak, trimmed and cut into 2 cm (3/4 inch) cubes
1 tablespoon oil
1 onion, chopped
30 g (1 oz) butter
1 tablespoon worcestershire sauce
1 tablespoon tomato paste (concentrated purée)
125 ml (4 fl oz/1/2 cup) red wine
250 ml (9 fl oz/1 cup) beef stock
125 g (4 1/2 oz) button mushrooms, sliced
1/2 teaspoon dried thyme
4 tablespoons chopped flat-leaf (Italian) parsley
500 g (1 lb 2 oz) block ready-made puff pastry, thawed
1 egg, lightly beaten

1 Peel the skin from the kidneys, quarter them and trim away any fat or sinew. Put the flour in a plastic bag with the beef and kidneys and toss gently. Heat the oil in a frying pan, add the onion and fry for 5 minutes, or until soft. Remove from the pan using a slotted spoon. Add the butter to the pan, brown the beef and kidneys in batches and then return the beef, kidneys and onion to the pan.

2 Add the worcestershire sauce, tomato paste, wine, stock, mushrooms and herbs to the pan. Bring to the boil, reduce the heat and simmer, covered, for 1 hour, or until the meat is tender. Season to taste and allow to cool. Spoon into a 1.5 litre (52 fl oz/ 6 cup) pie dish.

3 Preheat the oven to 210°C (415°F/ Gas 6–7). Roll the pastry between two sheets of baking paper, to a size 4 cm (1 1/2 inches) larger than the pie dish.

4 Cut thin strips from the edge of the pastry and press onto the rim of the dish, sealing the joins. Place the pastry on the pie, trim the edges and cut small holes in the top of the pastry to allow any steam to escape. Decorate the pie with leftover pastry and brush the top with egg. Bake for 35–40 minutes, or until the pastry is golden.

Caramelised tomato tart

SERVES 6–8 **PREPARATION TIME** 55 minutes (+ 50 minutes chilling & 15 minutes cooling) **COOKING TIME** 1 hour

1 quantity shortcrust pastry (see pages 16–17)
50 g (2½ oz/½ cup) finely grated parmesan cheese
9 (about 1 kg/2 lb 4 oz) firm, ripe roma (plum) tomatoes
30 g (1 oz) butter
1 tablespoon light brown sugar
1 tablespoon balsamic vinegar
1 egg yolk, lightly whisked
Sprigs of small marjoram leaves, to garnish

1 Make the pastry as directed, adding the parmesan after the butter has been rubbed in.

2 Cut a small cross in the base of each tomato. Bring a large saucepan of water to the boil. Add the tomatoes and cook for about 30 seconds or until the skins begin to peel away from the flesh. Drain and refresh under cold water. Peel the skins, then cut the tomatoes in half lengthways. Use a small spoon to carefully scrape the seeds and juice into a bowl, leaving the centre membranes as they will help the tomatoes hold their shape *(pic 1)*. Strain the seeds and juice through a fine sieve into a small jug. Discard the solids. Reserve the juice.

3 Melt the butter in a large frying pan over medium heat. Add the sugar and vinegar and cook, stirring, for 1 minute. Add the tomato halves and cook for 1–2 minutes, carefully turning once, or until softened slightly. Remove from the pan and set aside to cool completely. Add the reserved tomato juice to the pan and bring to the boil. Reduce the heat to low and simmer, uncovered, for 2 minutes or until reduced by half *(pic 2)*. Transfer to a small jug.

4 Meanwhile, use a lightly floured rolling pin to roll out the pastry on a lightly floured work surface to a rectangle, about 16 x 42 cm (6¼ x 16½ inches). Roll the pastry around the rolling pin and carefully ease into a 2 cm (¾ inch) deep, 12 x 35 cm (4½ x 14 inch) fluted loose-based tart (flan) tin, pressing it into the base and sides with your fingertips (see page 20). Roll the rolling pin over the tin to trim the excess pastry, then refrigerate for 20 minutes to chill.

5 Preheat the oven to 200°C (400°F/Gas 6). Line the pastry shell with non-stick baking paper and fill with baking beads, dried beans or uncooked rice. Bake for 20 minutes, reduce the temperature to 180°C (350°F/Gas 4) and remove the paper and weights. Brush the pastry base with egg yolk.

6 Return the tart shell to the oven and bake for a further 10 minutes or until the base is golden and dry. Arrange the tomatoes, cut side down, in the pastry shell *(pic 3)*. The tighter you pack them in, the better the result will be, as they will collapse a little during cooking.

7 Bake the tart for 20 minutes or until the pastry is cooked through. Leave in tin to cool for 15 minutes. Warm the reduced tomato juice. Serve drizzled with the tomato juice and sprinkled with the marjoram sprigs.

1

2

3

TIP This tart is best eaten on the day it is baked.

Onion tart

SERVES 4–6 **PREPARATION TIME** 30 minutes (+ 40 minutes chilling) **COOKING TIME** 1 hour 30 minutes

SHORTCRUST PASTRY

150 g (5½ oz/1¼ cups) plain (all-purpose) flour
90 g (3¼ oz) butter, chilled and cubed
2–3 tablespoons chilled water

FILLING

25 g (1 oz) butter
7 onions, sliced
1 tablespoon dijon mustard
3 eggs, lightly beaten
125 g (4½ oz/½ cup) sour cream
25 g (1 oz/¼ cup) freshly grated parmesan cheese
dressed rocket (arugula) leaves, to serve

1 Lightly grease a 23 cm (9 inch) round fluted flan (tart) tin. To make the pastry, sift the flour into a bowl. Using your fingertips, rub in the butter until the mixture resembles fine breadcrumbs. Make a well in the centre, add almost all the water and mix with a flat-bladed knife, using a cutting action, until the mixture comes together in beads. Add more water if the dough is too dry.

2 Gather the dough together and lift out onto a lightly floured work surface. Press together until smooth, wrap in plastic wrap and refrigerate for 20 minutes. Roll out between two sheets of baking paper large enough to cover the base and side of the tin. Place the pastry in the tin and trim the edge. Cover with plastic wrap and refrigerate for 20 minutes.

3 Preheat the oven to 180°C (350°F/Gas 4). Line the pastry case with baking paper and spread with baking beads or uncooked rice. Bake for 10 minutes, remove the paper and beads and bake for another 10 minutes. Cool completely.

4 To make the filling, melt the butter in a large heavy-based frying pan. Add the onion, cover and cook over medium heat for 25 minutes. Uncover and cook for another 10 minutes, stirring often. Cool.

5 Spread the mustard over the pastry, then top with the onion. Whisk together the eggs and sour cream and pour on top. Sprinkle with the parmesan and bake for 35 minutes, or until set. Serve with rocket.

Lemon tart

This is a gorgeous, silky smooth, lemony tart ideal for those who prefer a not-so-sweet dessert. Try replacing the lemon zest and juice with lime zest and juice for a slightly different flavour.

SERVES 8 **PREPARATION TIME** 30 minutes (+ 1 hour chilling) **COOKING TIME** 50 minutes

1 quantity sweet shortcrust pastry (see pages 16–17)
5 eggs, at room temperature
220 g (7¾ oz/1 cup) caster (superfine) sugar
Finely grated zest of 2 lemons
125 ml (4 fl oz/½ cup) strained freshly squeezed lemon juice
150 ml (5 fl oz) pouring (whipping) cream
Cream or vanilla ice cream, to serve

1 Use a lightly floured rolling pin to roll out the pastry on a lightly floured work surface to 4 mm (¼ inch) thick. (Alternatively, roll out the pastry between 2 sheets of non-stick baking paper.) Roll the pastry around the rolling pin and carefully ease it into a 2.5 cm (1 inch) deep, 24 cm (9½ inch) fluted, loose-based tart (flan) tin, pressing it into the edges with your fingertips (see page 20). Trim any excess pastry by rolling the rolling pin over the top of the tin. Cover with plastic wrap and place in the refrigerator for 30 minutes.

2 Preheat the oven to 200°C (400°F/Gas 6).

3 Line the pastry shell with non-stick baking paper and fill with baking beads, rice or beans. Bake for 10 minutes. Remove the beads or rice and paper and bake for a further 10 minutes or until light golden.

4 Just before the pastry shell is ready, prepare the filling. Use a balloon whisk to whisk together the eggs, sugar and lemon zest until well combined *(pic 1)*. Add the lemon juice and cream and gently whisk to combine. Strain the filling into a jug *(pic 2)*.

5 Remove the pastry shell from the oven and reduce the oven temperature to 180°C (350°F/Gas 4). Pour the filling into the hot pastry shell *(pic 3)*. Return to the oven and bake for 30 minutes or until just set in the centre. Cool the tart in the tin, placed on a wire rack. Serve with cream or vanilla ice cream.

1

2

3

TIP To really enjoy the fragrant lemon in this tart it is best made and served on the same day. It can, however, be stored in an airtight container in the refrigerator for up to 3 days. Bring to room temperature before serving.

Linzertorte

Arguably the oldest cake in the world (the word *torte* is German for 'cake'), the Linzertorte is from the town of Linz in Austria. It always uses ground almonds in the pastry, has a lattice pattern on top, and is filled with jam (traditionally, redcurrant jam).

SERVES 10 **PREPARATION TIME** 40 minutes (+ 30 minutes chilling) **COOKING TIME** 48 minutes

160 g (5¾ oz/1 cup) almonds
300 g (10½ oz/2 cups) plain (all-purpose) flour
1 teaspoon baking powder
2½ teaspoons ground cinnamon
½ teaspoon ground cloves
250 g (9 oz) unsalted butter, softened
220 g (7¾ oz/1 cup) caster (superfine) sugar
1 teaspoon natural vanilla extract
Finely grated zest of 1 orange
2 egg yolks
500 g (1 lb 2 oz) raspberry jam
1 egg yolk, extra, lightly whisked
2½ tablespoons flaked almonds

1 Preheat the oven to 180°C (350°F/Gas 4). Spread the almonds on a baking tray and toast for 8 minutes or until aromatic. Set aside to cool. Transfer to a food processor and process until finely ground *(pic 1)*.

2 Sift the flour, baking powder and spices into a bowl. Use an electric mixer to beat the butter, sugar, vanilla and orange zest in a separate medium bowl until pale and creamy. Add the egg yolks one at a time, beating well after each addition. Add the flour mixture and ground toasted almonds and use a flat-bladed knife, then your hands, to mix until a soft dough forms.

3 Turn the dough out onto a lightly floured work surface and shape into a disc. Wrap in plastic wrap and refrigerate for 30 minutes.

4 Preheat the oven to 180°C (350°F/Gas 4). Divide the dough into 3 portions, then combine 2 of them. Use a lightly floured rolling pin to roll out the larger portion on a lightly floured work surface to a 30 cm (12 inch) round, taking care not to work the dough too much as it will become very soft. Roll the pastry around the rolling pin and carefully ease it into a 2 cm (¾ inch) deep, 24 cm (9½ inch) fluted, loose-based tart (flan) tin, pressing it into the edges with your fingertips (see page 20). Trim any excess by rolling the rolling pin over the top of the tin.

5 Spread the jam into the pastry shell to cover the base evenly. Roll the remaining dough out between 2 sheets of non-stick baking paper to a rectangle about 20 x 26 cm (8 x 10½ inches) and about 5 mm (¼ inch) thick. Use a fluted pastry wheel or a large sharp knife to cut the remaining portion of dough into 1.5 cm (⅝ inch) wide strips *(pic 2)*. Arrange the strips over the jam to form a lattice pattern *(pic 3)*, taking care as the dough will be quite fragile and may break easily. Re-roll any scraps as necessary to make enough strips to form the lattice.

6 Use a small sharp knife to trim the edges of the strips. Lightly brush the strips with the extra egg yolk and sprinkle the tart with flaked almonds.

7 Bake for 40 minutes or until deep golden and the pastry is cooked through. Leave in the tin to cool. Serve at room temperature.

1

2

3

TIP Keep the linzertorte in an airtight container for up to 3 days.

Deep-dish apple pie

SERVES 8 **PREPARATION TIME** 1 hour (+ 40 minutes chilling) **COOKING TIME** 1 hour

250 g (9 oz/2 cups) plain (all-purpose) flour
30 g (1 oz/¼ cup) self-raising flour
150 g (5½ oz) unsalted butter, chilled and cubed
2 tablespoons caster (superfine) sugar
4–5 tablespoons iced water
1 egg, lightly beaten, for glazing

FILLING
8 large granny smith apples
2 thick strips lemon zest
6 whole cloves
1 cinnamon stick
125 g (4½ oz/½ cup) sugar

1 Lightly grease a deep 20 cm (8 inch) spring-form tin. Line the base with baking paper and grease the paper, then dust lightly with flour and shake off the excess.

2 Sift the flours into a bowl and rub in the butter with your fingertips until the mixture resembles fine breadcrumbs. Mix in the sugar, then make a well in the centre. Add almost all the water and mix with a flat-bladed knife, using a cutting action, until the mixture comes together in beads. Add more water if necessary. Gather together on a floured surface. Wrap in plastic wrap and refrigerate for 20 minutes.

3 Roll two-thirds of the pastry between two sheets of baking paper until large enough to cover the base and side of the tin. Line the tin with the pastry. Roll out the remaining pastry between the baking paper sheets to fit the top of the tin. Refrigerate the pastry for 20 minutes.

4 To make the filling, peel and core the apples and cut each into 12 wedges. Combine with the lemon zest, cloves, cinnamon, sugar and 500 ml (17 fl oz/2 cups) water in a large saucepan. Cover and simmer for 10 minutes, or until tender. Drain well and set aside to cool. Discard the zest, cloves and cinnamon.

5 Preheat the oven to 180°C (350°F/Gas 4). Spoon the apple into the pastry shell. Brush the pastry edges with beaten egg and cover with the pastry top. Trim with a sharp knife, crimping the edges to seal. Prick the top with a fork and brush with beaten egg. Bake for 50 minutes, or until the pastry is cooked. Leave in the tin for 10 minutes before removing to serve.

Rich chocolate tart

This luscious, not-too-sweet tart is best made using a semi-sweet chocolate for the ganache filling. Don't let plastic wrap or any other covering touch the surface of the ganache filling when chilling the tart or it will lose its beautiful sheen.

SERVES 10 **PREPARATION TIME** 30 minutes (+ 4 hours chilling & 30 minutes cooling) **COOKING TIME** 25 minutes

1 quantity chocolate pâte sucrée (see page 19)
Dutch unsweetened cocoa powder, to dust (optional)
Double (thick/heavy) cream or vanilla or coffee ice cream, to serve

CHOCOLATE GANACHE FILLING
300 g (10½ oz) dark chocolate (70% cocoa solids), chopped
310 ml (10¾ fl oz/1¼ cups) pouring (whipping) cream
60 ml (2 fl oz/¼ cup) brandy, dark rum or Frangelico

1 Use a lightly floured rolling pin to roll out the pastry on a cool, lightly floured work surface to a large rectangle, about 22 x 45 cm (8½ x 17¾ inches) and 3 mm (⅛ inch) thick.

2 Line an 11.5 x 34.5 cm (4½ x 13¾ inch) tart (flan) tin (base measurement) with a removable base *(pic 1)* with the pastry, gently easing it into the tin with your fingertips and making sure it fits snugly against the sides and on the base (see page 20). Trim any overhanging pastry by rolling the rolling pin over the top of the tin. Place on a baking tray and refrigerate for 30 minutes or until it is well chilled.

3 Preheat the oven to 200°C (400°F/Gas 6).

4 Line the pastry shell with non-stick baking paper and fill with baking beads, dried beans or uncooked rice. Bake for 10 minutes. Remove the paper and weights, reduce the oven temperature to 180°C (350°F/Gas 4) and bake for a further 15 minutes or until cooked through and dry to the touch. Remove from the oven, place on a wire rack and cool to room temperature.

5 o make the chocolate ganache filling, put the chocolate in a medium heatproof bowl. Place the cream in a small saucepan and bring just to a simmer. Pour the hot cream over the chocolate *(pic 2)* and stand for 2 minutes. Stir until the chocolate melts and the mixture is completely smooth. Stir in the brandy, rum or Frangelico, then set aside for 30 minutes, stirring occasionally, until the ganache has cooled to room temperature.

6 Pour the ganache filling into the cooled tart shell *(pic 3)*, then gently tap the tin on the bench to even the surface (don't smooth with the back of a spoon or a spatula as it will leave streaks over the surface of the tart). Refrigerate for 3 hours or until the filling is set.

7 Dust the tart with the cocoa, if using. Use a warmed, dry knife to cut the tart into thick slices and serve accompanied by cream or ice cream.

1

2

3

Free-form blueberry pie

SERVES 4 **PREPARATION TIME** 30 minutes **COOKING TIME** 35 minutes

185 g (6½ oz/1½ cups) plain (all-purpose) flour
90 g (3¼ oz/¾ cup) icing (confectioners') sugar, plus extra, for dusting
125 g (4½ oz) unsalted butter, chilled and cubed
60 ml (2 fl oz/¼ cup) lemon juice
500 g (1 lb 2 oz) blueberries
1 teaspoon finely grated lemon zest
½ teaspoon ground cinnamon
1 egg white, lightly beaten
ice cream or whipped cream, to serve

1 Preheat the oven to 180°C (350°F/Gas 4). Sift together the flour and 60 g (2¼ oz/½ cup) of the icing sugar into a bowl. Using your fingertips, rub in the butter until the mixture resembles fine breadcrumbs. Make a well in the centre and add almost the lemon juice. Mix with a flat-bladed knife, using a cutting action, until the mixture comes together in beads. Add the remaining lemon juice if the dough is too dry.

2 Gently gather the dough together and lift onto a sheet of baking paper. Roll the dough out to a circle about 30 cm (12 inches) in diameter. Wrap in plastic wrap and refrigerate for 10 minutes. Put the blueberries in a bowl and sprinkle with the remaining icing sugar, lemon zest and cinnamon.

3 Place the pastry (still on the baking paper) on a baking tray. Brush the centre lightly with beaten egg white. Pile the blueberry mixture onto the pastry in a 20 cm (8 inch) diameter circle, then fold the edges of the pastry over the filling, leaving the centre uncovered. Bake for 30–35 minutes, until the pastry is golden brown. Dust the pie generously with icing sugar and serve warm with ice cream or whipped cream.

TIP Buy firm, dry and unblemished blueberries with their natural whitish 'bloom' still evident. Store them unwashed and in their container. They can be refrigerated for up to two days and can be used for pies, tarts, muffins, jam and fruit salads.

Lemon meringue pie

SERVES 8–10 **PREPARATION TIME** 30 minutes (+ 4 hours chilling and 30 minutes cooling) **COOKING TIME** 1 hour

1 quantity sweet shortcrust pastry (see pages 16–17)

LEMON FILLING
10 egg yolks, at room temperature
220 g (7¾ oz/1 cup) caster (superfine) sugar
Finely grated zest of 3 lemons
40 g (1½ oz/⅓ cup) cornflour (cornstarch)
160 ml (5¼ fl oz/⅔ cup) strained, freshly squeezed lemon juice
200 g (7 oz) unsalted butter, chilled and cut into 1 cm (½ inch) dice

ITALIAN MERINGUE
165 g (5¾ oz/¾ cup) caster (superfine) sugar
3 egg whites, at room temperature
Pinch of cream of tartar

1 Preheat the oven to 180°C (350°F/Gas 4). Use a lightly floured rolling pin to roll out the pastry on a lightly floured work surface to a 4 mm (⅛ inch) thick round. Ease it into a 22 cm (8½ inch) diameter, 4.5 cm (1¾ inch) deep pie tin, making sure it fits snugly, then trim the excess. Refrigerate for 20 minutes.

2 Line the pastry shell with non-stick baking paper and fill with baking beads, dried beans or uncooked rice. Bake for 20 minutes, then remove the paper and weights and bake for 20–25 minutes or until golden and cooked through. Cool to room temperature on a wire rack.

3 Invert the pastry onto your hand, then place on a baking tray. To make the lemon filling, place the egg yolks, sugar and lemon zest in a saucepan and use a balloon whisk to whisk until well combined. Combine the cornflour with 125 ml (4 fl oz/½ cup) water. Add to the pan with the lemon juice and whisk to combine. Add the butter. Place over medium heat and whisk constantly for 2 minutes or until the butter has melted. Continue whisking for 3–4 minutes or until thick and almost boiling (do not allow it to boil) *(pic 1)*. Immediately pour it into the pastry shell and use a palette knife dipped in boiling water to spread to the edges (see tip). Cool, then refrigerate for 3 hours or until set.

4 To make the Italian meringue, combine the sugar with 80 ml (2½ fl oz/⅓ cup) water in a small saucepan and stir over medium heat until the sugar dissolves. Brush down the side of the pan with a pastry brush dipped in water to remove any sugar crystals. Increase the heat to high and bring to the boil. Cook, brushing down the pan occasionally *(pic 2)*, until the mixture reaches thread stage (110°C/230°F) on a sugar thermometer. At this point, put the egg whites and cream of tartar in a medium bowl and use an electric mixer with a whisk attachment to whisk on medium–high speed until soft peaks form. Continue cooking the sugar syrup until it reaches hard ball stage (118°C/244°F), then, with the motor running on high, gradually pour it onto the egg whites in a steady stream. Whisk constantly for 6–7 minutes, until the meringue is very thick and glossy, and has cooled to room temperature.

5 Preheat the grill (broiler) to medium. Spoon the meringue over the filling and use a palette knife to spread, swirling as you go *(pic 3)*. Put on the middle shelf of the oven and grill for 30 seconds. Check the colour and grill for 30 seconds more if needed, turning the pie if it's colouring unevenly. Stand for 5 minutes. Use a sharp knife dipped in very hot water and dried to cut the pie into slices.

1

2

3

Treacle tart

SERVES 4-6 **PREPARATION TIME** 20 minutes (+ 40 minutes chilling time) **COOKING TIME** 35 minutes

Icing (confectioners') sugar and vanilla ice cream, to serve

SHORTCRUST PASTRY

150 g (5½ oz/1¼ cups) plain (all-purpose) flour
90 g (3¼ oz) unsalted butter, chilled and cubed
2–3 tablespoons chilled water
1 egg, lightly beaten, to glaze

FILLING

350 g (12 oz/1 cup) light treacle or golden syrup
25 g (1 oz) unsalted butter
½ teaspoon ground ginger
140 g (5 oz/1¾ cups) fresh white breadcrumbs

1 To make the pastry, sift the flour into a large bowl. Using your fingertips, rub in the butter until the mixture resembles fine breadcrumbs. Add almost all the water and mix with a flat-bladed knife, using a cutting action, to a firm dough. Add more water if the dough is too dry. Turn onto a lightly floured surface and gather into a ball. Wrap in plastic wrap and refrigerate for 20 minutes.

2 Lightly brush a 20 cm (8 inch) round fluted flan (tart) tin with melted butter or oil. Roll out the pastry large enough to fit the base and side of the tin, allowing a 4 cm (1½ inch) overhang. Ease the pastry into the tin and trim by running a rolling pin firmly across the top of the tin. Re-roll the pastry trimmings to a 10 x 20 cm (4 x 8 inch) rectangle. Using a sharp knife or fluted pastry wheel, cut into long strips 1 cm (½ inch) wide. Cover the pastry case and strips with plastic wrap and refrigerate for 20 minutes. Preheat the oven to 180°C (350°F/Gas 4).

3 To make the filling, combine the treacle or golden syrup, butter and ginger in a small saucepan and stir over low heat until the butter melts. Stir in the breadcrumbs until combined. Pour the mixture into the pastry case. Lay half the pastry strips over the tart, starting at the centre and working outwards. Lay the remaining strips over the tart to form a lattice pattern. Brush the lattice with the beaten egg. Bake the tart for 30 minutes, or until the pastry is lightly golden. Serve warm or at room temperature. Dust the top with icing sugar and serve with vanilla ice cream.

Tarte tatin

The Tatin sisters, who ran a hotel in France in the early 1900s, created this upside-down tart. It is traditionally made with apples, though pears are a common substitute.

SERVES 10 **PREPARATION TIME** 30 minutes (+ 4 hours chilling & 30 minutes cooling) **COOKING TIME** 25 minutes

- **3 large (600 g/1 lb 5 oz) granny smith apples**
- **75 g (2¾ oz) unsalted butter, chopped**
- **150 g (5½ oz/⅔ cup) caster (superfine) sugar**
- **1 sheet (24 x 24 cm/9½ x 9½ inches) frozen butter puff pastry, thawed slightly (see tip)**
- **Crème fraîche, thick (double/heavy) cream, pouring custard or ice cream, to serve**

1 Peel, core and halve the apples. Cut each apple half into 3 wedges. Combine the butter and sugar in a 21 cm (8¼ inch) (base measurement) ovenproof cast-iron pan and place over medium heat. Cook, stirring occasionally, for 5 minutes or until the butter has melted and the mixture is bubbling. Remove from the heat and arrange the apple wedges over the base of the pan *(pic 1)*. You may have some apple left over.

2 Return the pan to medium heat and cook for 15 minutes or until the apples are tender and golden underneath *(pic 2)*. Remove the pan from the heat and allow the apple mixture to cool completely. Preheat the oven to 180°C (350°F/Gas 4).

3 Cut the pastry into a 24 cm (9½ inch) round. Place the pastry over the cooled apples, then carefully tuck it around the apples, pushing it gently down the inside of the pan and onto the apples *(pic 3)*. Bake for 40–45 minutes or until the pastry is deep golden and cooked through, and the apple juices are bubbling. Remove from the oven and set aside for 10 minutes to cool slightly.

4 Invert the tarte tatin onto a serving plate. Serve immediately, cut into wedges, with crème fraîche, cream, pouring custard or ice cream.

VARIATION

Pear and honey tarte tatin: Use 4 firm, ripe beurre bosc or william pears instead of the apples. Peel, core and cut the pears into quarters. Replace half the sugar with 115 g (4 oz/⅓ cup) honey.

1

2

3

TIP You can use 1 quantity sweet shortcrust pastry (see pages 24–24), rolled out to 5 mm (¼ inch) thick and cut into a 24 cm (9½ inch) round instead of puff pastry.

Bramble pie

SERVES 4-6 **PREPARATION TIME** 20 minutes (+ 40 minutes chilling time) **COOKING TIME** 35 minutes

125 g (4½ oz/1 cup) self-raising flour
125 g (4½ oz/1 cup) plain (all-purpose) flour
2 tablespoons caster (superfine) sugar
125 g (4½ oz) cold unsalted butter, chopped
1 egg, lightly beaten
3–4 tablespoons milk

FILLING
2 tablespoons cornflour (cornstarch)
2–4 tablespoons caster (superfine) sugar, to taste
1 teaspoon grated orange zest
1 tablespoon orange juice
600 g (1 lb 5 oz) brambles (see Note)

GLAZE
1 egg yolk, mixed with 1 teaspoon water

1 Sift the flours into a large bowl and add the sugar. Using your fingertips, lightly rub in the butter until the mixture resembles fine breadcrumbs. Make a well in the centre, then add the egg and most of the milk to the well. Mix using a flat-bladed knife until a rough dough forms, adding a little more milk if necessary. Turn out onto a lightly floured work surface, then gently press together into a ball. Form into a flat disc, cover with plastic wrap and refrigerate for 30 minutes.

2 Meanwhile, preheat the oven to 180°C (350°F/Gas 4).

3 To make the filling, combine the cornflour, sugar, orange zest and orange juice in a saucepan. Add half the berries and stir over low heat for 5 minutes, or until the mixture boils and thickens. Leave to cool, then stir in the remaining berries.

4 Pour into a 750 ml (26 fl oz/3 cup) pie dish.

5 Cut the chilled dough in half. Roll out one portion on a lightly floured work surface until large enough to cover the top of the dish, trimming away the excess. Roll out the other half and, using heart-shaped pastry cutters of various sizes, cut out some hearts to decorate the pie. Brush the pie with the glaze and bake for 35 minutes, or until golden brown. Serve hot or warm.

NOTE: Brambles include any creeping stem berries, such as boysenberries, blackberries, loganberries and youngberries. You can use just one variety or a combination.

Bramble pie is best eaten the day it is made.

Pistachio and fig tart

Frangipane is a traditional French tart filling, invented by a 16th century cook of the same name, or so the story goes. It is made using finely ground almonds, although hazelnuts or pistachios, as used here, are delicious alternatives.

SERVES 8–10 **PREPARATION TIME** 35 minutes (+ 1 hour chilling & 30 minutes standing) **COOKING TIME** 55–60 minutes

1 quantity pâte sucrée (see page 19)
6 firm ripe figs (85 g/3 oz each)
Icing (confectioners') sugar, to dust
Thick (double/heavy) cream, vanilla ice cream or pouring custard, to serve

PISTACHIO & ROSEWATER FRANGIPANE
250 g (9 oz) unsalted pistachios
2 tablespoons plain (all-purpose) flour
125 g (4½ oz) unsalted butter, at room temperature
110 g (3¾ oz/½ cup) caster (superfine) sugar
3 eggs
1½ teaspoons rosewater, or to taste
50 g (1¾ oz/½ cup) flaked almonds

1 Remove the pastry from the refrigerator and set aside at room temperature for 20–30 minutes or until slightly pliable. Use a lightly floured rolling pin to roll out the pastry on a cool, lightly floured work surface to a round about 3 mm (⅛ inch) thick. Gently ease the pastry into a round 28 cm (11¼ inch) fluted loose-based tart (flan) tin, making sure it fits snugly against the side and on the base (see page 20). Trim any overhanging pastry by rolling the rolling pin over the top of the tin. Place on a baking tray and refrigerate for 30 minutes.

2 Meanwhile, preheat the oven to 200°C (400°F/Gas 6). Line the pastry shell with non-stick baking paper and fill with baking beads, dried beans or uncooked rice. Bake for 10 minutes, then remove the paper and weights. Reduce the oven temperature to 180°C (350°F/Gas 4) and bake the pastry shell for a further 10 minutes. Transfer to a wire rack and cool to room temperature.

3 Cut each fig into 8 wedges and arrange over the cooled pastry *(pic 1)*.

4 To make the pistachio and rosewater frangipane, put the pistachios and flour in a food processor bowl and process until the nuts are very finely ground. Use an electric mixer to beat the butter and sugar in a medium mixing bowl until pale and creamy. Add the eggs one at a time, beating well after each addition. Add the pistachio mixture and rosewater and stir until well combined. Carefully spread the frangipane over the figs to cover *(pic 2)*. Scatter the almonds evenly over the frangipane.

5 Bake for 35–40 minutes or until the frangipane is cooked through and the tart is golden. Transfer to a wire rack and cool to room temperature.

6 Dust the tart with icing sugar *(pic 3)*. Cut into wedges and serve with cream, vanilla ice cream or pouring custard.

1

2

3

TIP This tart is best eaten on the day it is baked.

Double-crust apple pie

This traditional apple pie has a melt-in-the-mouth pastry shell and sweet apple filling, thickened with almond meal and given a slight tang by the addition of lemon juice. It's comfort cooking at its best.

SERVES 8 **PREPARATION TIME** 40 minutes (+ 30 minutes chilling, and cooling) **COOKING TIME** 50 minutes

2 quantities sweet shortcrust pastry (see pages 16–17)
1 egg, lightly whisked
1 tablespoon sugar, to sprinkle
Vanilla ice cream or pouring (whipping) cream, to serve

FILLING
1.2 kg (2 lb 10 oz) granny smith apples
2 tablespoons lemon juice
25 g (1 oz/¼ cup) almond meal
110 g (3¾ oz/½ cup) sugar
1 teaspoon ground cinnamon
¼ teaspoon ground nutmeg
Finely grated zest of 1 lemon

1 Make the 2 quantities of pastry separately and place in the refrigerator to rest, as directed.

2 To make the filling, peel the apples, cut into quarters and cut away the core. Slice each quarter into wedges about 2 cm (¾ inch) thick. Put the apples in a large, deep frying pan with the lemon juice, cover with a tight-fitting lid and cook over medium–low heat, stirring occasionally, for 5–7 minutes or until just soft. Transfer the apples to a colander and set aside to drain and cool to room temperature.

3 Meanwhile, use a rolling pin to roll out each pastry disc between 2 sheets of non-stick baking paper to 3 mm (⅛ inch) thick. Place one portion on a large baking tray, still between the baking paper, and refrigerate until required. Use the remaining pastry to line a 4.5 cm (1¾ inch) deep, round 22 cm (8½ inch) pie tin, easing it gently into the base (see page 20) and allowing it to overhang the top edge (do not trim). Place on a baking tray and refrigerate until required.

4 Preheat the oven to 200°C (400°F/Gas 6). When the apples have cooled, remove the pastry shell and the rolled pastry from the refrigerator. Sprinkle the almond meal over the base of the pastry shell. Put the apples in a large bowl, add the combined sugar and spices and the lemon zest and gently fold through to combine.

5 Spoon the apple mixture into the pastry shell, then brush the edges of the pastry with the egg *(pic 1)*. Peel the paper away from the rolled pastry and invert the pastry on top of the pie, over the apples. Remove the paper on top and gently press the edges of the pastry to seal *(pic 2)*, then trim with a sharp knife around the outside edge of the tin. Press and fold the pastry back inside the rim of the tin. Brush the top with egg and sprinkle with the sugar. Cut a small cross in the top of the pie to allow steam to escape *(pic 3)*.

6 Bake for 25 minutes, then turn the pie around in the oven to ensure even cooking and bake for a further 20 minutes or until the pastry is cooked through and deep golden. Serve warm with vanilla ice cream or cream.

1

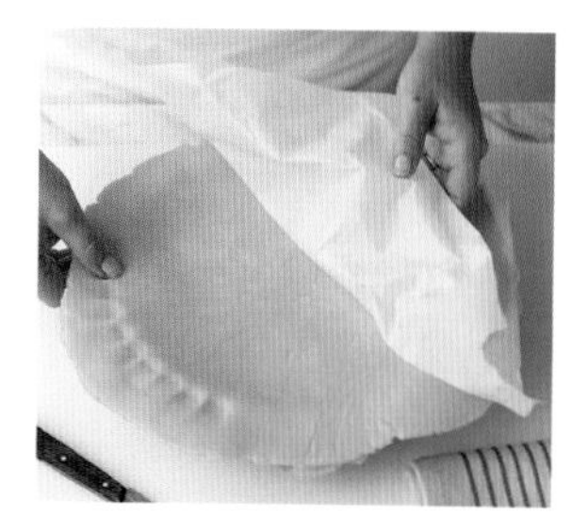
2

3

Citron tart

SERVES 6 **PREPARATION TIME** 30 minutes (+ 30 minutes chilling) **COOKING TIME** 1 hour

3 eggs
2 egg yolks
175 g (6 oz/3/4 cup) caster (superfine) sugar
125 ml (4 fl oz/1/2 cup) pouring (whipping) cream
185 ml (6 fl oz/3/4 cup) lemon juice
1 1/2 tablespoons finely grated lemon zest
2 small lemons
140 g (5 oz/2/3 cup) sugar
Pouring (whipping) cream (optional), to serve

PASTRY
125 g (4 1/2 oz/1 cup) plain (all-purpose) flour
80 g (2 3/4 oz) unsalted butter, softened
1 egg yolk
2 tablespoons icing (confectioners') sugar, sifted

1 To make the pastry, sift the flour and a pinch of salt into a large bowl. Make a well in the centre and add the butter, egg yolk and icing sugar. Work together the butter, yolk and sugar with your fingertips, then slowly incorporate the flour. Bring together into a ball — you may need to add a few drops of chilled water. Flatten the ball slightly, then wrap in plastic wrap and refrigerate for 20 minutes.

2 Preheat the oven to 200°C (400°F/Gas 6). Lightly grease a 21 cm (8 1/4 inch) round fluted flan (tart) tin.

3 Roll out the pastry between two sheets of baking paper until it is 3 mm (1/8 inch) thick, to fit the base and side of the tin. Gently place in the tin and trim the edge. Refrigerate for 10 minutes. Line the pastry with baking paper, fill with baking beads or uncooked rice and bake for 10 minutes. Remove the paper and beads and bake for another 6–8 minutes, or until the pastry looks dry all over. Allow to cool. Reduce the oven to 150°C (300°F/Gas 2).

4 Whisk the eggs, egg yolks and caster sugar together. Add the cream and lemon juice and mix well. Strain and then add the lemon zest. Place the tin on a baking tray on the middle shelf of the oven and carefully pour in the filling right up to the top. Bake for 40 minutes, or until it is just set — it should wobble in the middle when the tin is firmly tapped. Cool the tart before removing from the tin.

5 Meanwhile, wash and scrub the lemons well to remove the wax from the skin. Slice very thinly (2 mm/1/16 inch thick). Combine the sugar and 200 ml (7 fl oz) water in a small frying pan and stir over low heat until the sugar has dissolved. Add the lemon slices and simmer over low heat for 40 minutes, or until the peel is very tender and the pith looks translucent. Lift out of the syrup and drain on baking paper. If serving the tart immediately, cover the surface with the lemon slices. If not, keep the lemon slices covered and decorate the tart when ready to serve. You can serve the tart warm or chilled, with a little cream, if desired.

Free-form apple and rhubarb tart

Crisp buttery pastry encasing a slightly tart fruit filling is a superb combination and you'll come back to this recipe often. The fact that there are no special tin requirements, as the pastry is simply folded over the filling, is less intimidating for pastry novices, too. It's best served straight from the oven.

SERVES 6–8 **PREPARATION TIME** 30 minutes (+ 1 hour chilling) **COOKING TIME** 50–55 minutes

2 medium (about 300 g/10½ oz) apples (such as granny smith or golden delicious)
20 g (¾ oz) butter
2 tablespoons light brown sugar
1 tablespoon orange juice
4 rhubarb stalks, trimmed, cut into 5 cm (2 inch) lengths

1 quantity brown sugar shortcrust pastry (see page 17)
1 tablespoon raw sugar
Vanilla custard or ice cream, to serve

1 Preheat the oven to 200°C (400°F/Gas 6).

2 Peel and core the apples, then cut into thin wedges. Melt the butter in a medium frying pan over medium heat. Add the apples and cook, turning occasionally, for 2–3 minutes or until light golden. Add the brown sugar and orange juice and cook, stirring, for 1 minute or until the sugar dissolves. Add the rhubarb and cook, stirring, for 2–3 minutes or until the rhubarb starts to soften *(pic 1)*. Set aside to cool to room temperature.

3 Use a lightly floured rolling pin to roll the pastry out on a piece of non-stick baking paper to a 30 cm (12 inch) round, about 4 mm (1/4 inch) thick. Transfer the pastry, still on the paper, to a large baking tray. Spread the fruit mixture over the pastry, leaving a 4 cm (1½ inch) border around the edge (pic 2). Fold the border up and over the filling (pic 3). Sprinkle the upturned pastry edge with the raw sugar. Place the tart in the fridge for 20 minutes for the pastry to firm up slightly.

4 Bake the tart for 40–45 minutes or until the pastry is golden and crisp. Serve cut into wedges and accompanied by the custard or ice cream.

1

2

3

Bakewell tart

SERVES 6 **PREPARATION TIME** 45 minutes **COOKING TIME** 55 minutes

125 g (4½ oz/1 cup) plain (all-purpose) flour
90 g (3¼ oz) unsalted butter, chilled and cubed
2 teaspoons caster (superfine) sugar
2 tablespoons iced water
Icing (confectioners') sugar, to dust

FILLING
90 g (3¼ oz) unsalted butter, softened
80 g (2¾ oz/⅓ cup) caster (superfine) sugar
2 eggs, lightly beaten
3 drops natural almond extract
70 g (2½ oz/⅔ cup) ground almonds
40 g (1½ oz/⅓ cup) self-raising flour, sifted
160 g (5¾ oz/½ cup) raspberry jam

1 Preheat the oven to 180°C (350°F/Gas 4). Lightly grease a 20 cm (8 inch) loose-based, fluted flan (tart) tin.

2 Sift the flour into a large bowl and rub in the butter, using your fingertips, until the mixture resembles fine breadcrumbs. Stir in the caster sugar. Make a well in the centre, add almost all the water and mix with a flat-bladed knife, using a cutting action, until the mixture comes together in beads, adding more water if it is too dry. Gently gather the dough together and roll out between two sheets of baking paper to cover the base and side of the tin. Line the tin with the pastry, trim the edges and refrigerate for 20 minutes.

3 Line the pastry with baking paper and spread a layer of baking beads or uncooked rice over the paper. Bake for 10 minutes, then remove the paper and beads and bake the pastry for a further 7 minutes, or until golden. Leave to cool.

4 To make the filling, beat the butter and sugar in a small bowl using electric beaters until light and creamy. Add the egg gradually, beating thoroughly after each addition. Add the almond extract and beat until combined. Transfer to a large bowl and fold in the almonds and flour with a metal spoon. Spread the jam over the pastry, then spoon the almond mixture on top and smooth the surface. Bake for 35 minutes, or until risen and golden. Dust with icing sugar.

Peach pie

SERVES 8–10 **PREPARATION TIME** 40 minutes (+ 1 hour chilling) **COOKING TIME** 1 hour

850 g (1 lb 14 oz) yellow peaches
110 g (3¾ oz/½ cup) caster (superfine) sugar
45 g (1¾ oz/⅓ cup) slivered almonds
Whipped cream, to serve

SHORTCAKE PASTRY
175 g (6 oz) unsalted butter, softened
110 g (3¾ oz/½ cup) caster (superfine) sugar
1½ teaspoons natural vanilla extract
1 egg, lightly whisked
260 g (9¼ oz/1¾ cups) self-raising flour
80 g (2¾ oz/¾ cup) almond meal

1 To make the shortcake pastry, use an electric mixer to beat the butter and sugar in a medium bowl until pale and creamy. Add the vanilla and egg and beat until well combined. Combine the flour and almond meal in a bowl, add to the butter mixture and stir with a wooden spoon, and then your hands, until well combined. Shape into a disc, wrap in plastic wrap and refrigerate for 1 hour or until firm.

2 Meanwhile, cut the peach flesh from the stones. Chop the flesh into 1 cm (½ inch) pieces, then put in a medium saucepan with the sugar and 60 ml (2 fl oz/¼ cup) water. Cover and cook over medium heat, stirring occasionally, for 15 minutes or until the peaches are very tender *(pic 1)*.

3 Transfer the peach mixture to a sieve set over a bowl to drain, reserving the juices. Put the peaches in a heatproof bowl and set aside. Pour the cooking liquid into a small saucepan. Boil for 5 minutes or until thick and syrupy. Add to the peaches, then refrigerate for 20 minutes or until cooled to room temperature.

4 Preheat the oven to 180°C (350°F/Gas 4). Lightly brush a 9.5 cm x 33.5 cm (3¾ x 13¼ inch) (base measurement) fluted loose-based tart (flan) tin with melted butter to grease.

5 Divide the pastry into 3 portions. Wrap one portion in plastic wrap and return to the refrigerator. Combine the remaining portions. Pinch off small amounts of pastry and press into the greased tin to evenly line the sides and base *(pic 2)* (it should be about 5 mm/¼ inch thick). Roll a rolling pin over the top of the tin to trim any excess pastry.

6 Spoon the cooled peach mixture evenly into the pastry shell. Coarsely grate the reserved chilled pastry over the peach filling to cover evenly *(pic 3)*. Sprinkle with the almonds.

7 Bake for 35 minutes or until the pastry is golden and cooked through. Transfer to a wire rack and cool to room temperature. Slice and serve with the whipped cream.

1

2

3

TIP This pastry is simple to make and perfect to use when the pie filling is slightly wet, as in this recipe. Try using it in your favourite pie and tart recipes.

You can add 2½ teaspoons finely chopped rosemary to the flour and almond meal when making the pastry if you wish.

This pie is also delicious accompanied by pouring custard.

Rhubarb lattice pie

SERVES 4–6 **PREPARATION TIME** 35 minutes (+ 40 minutes chilling time) **COOKING TIME** 1 hour

150 g (5½ oz/1¼ cups) plain (all-purpose) flour
¼ teaspoon baking powder
90 g (3¼ oz) unsalted butter, chilled and cubed
1 tablespoon caster (superfine) sugar
80–100 ml (2½–3½ fl oz) iced water
milk, to glaze
raw (demerara) sugar, to decorate

RHUBARB FILLING
500 g (1 lb 2 oz) rhubarb, trimmed, leaves discarded
115 g (4 oz/½ cup) caster (superfine) sugar, plus extra, to taste
5 cm (2 inch) piece orange zest, pith removed
1 tablespoon orange juice
410 g (14½ oz) tinned pie apple, drained

1 To make the rhubarb filling, preheat the oven to 180°C (350°F/Gas 4). Cut the rhubarb into 3 cm (1¼ inch) lengths and combine in a large casserole dish with the sugar, orange zest and juice. Cover the dish with a lid or foil and bake for 30 minutes, or until the rhubarb is just tender. Drain away any excess juice and discard the zest. Cool, then stir in the apple. Add more sugar to taste.

2 While the rhubarb is cooking, sift the flour and baking powder into a bowl. Using your fingertips, rub in the butter until the mixture resembles fine breadcrumbs. Stir in the sugar. Make a well in the centre and add almost all the water. Mix with a flat-bladed knife, using a cutting action, until the mixture comes together in beads. Add more water if the dough is too dry. Gather together, wrap in plastic wrap and chill for 20 minutes.

3 Roll the pastry out between two sheets of baking paper to a 28 cm (11¼ inch) circle (*pic 1*). Use a sharp knife or a fluted cutter to cut the pastry into 1.5 cm (⅝ inch) strips. Lay half the strips on a sheet of baking paper, leaving a 1 cm (½ inch) gap between each strip. Interweave the remaining strips to form a lattice. Cover with plastic wrap and refrigerate, flat, for 20 minutes.

4 Increase the oven to 210°C (415°F/Gas 6–7). Pour the filling into a 20 cm (8 inch) pie dish and smooth the surface (*pic 2*). Invert the pastry lattice on the pie, remove the paper and trim the pastry edge. Bake for 10 minutes. Remove from the oven, brush with milk and sprinkle with sugar. Reduce the oven to 180°C (350°F/Gas 4) and bake the pie for a further 20 minutes, or until the pastry is golden and the filling is bubbling.

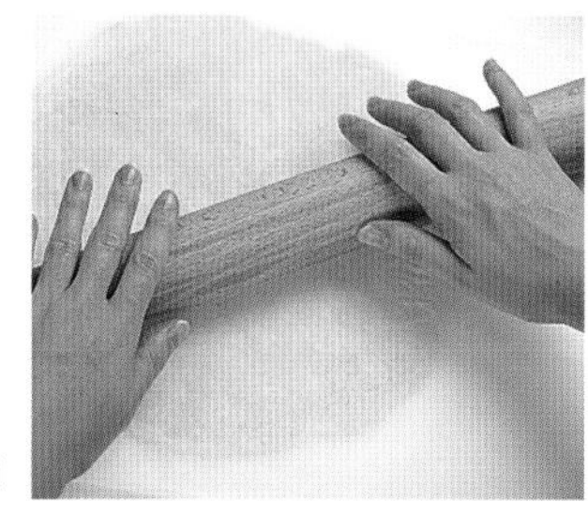
1

2

Pecan pie

The pecan nut is native to the Americas and was an important food source in pre-colonial times. Its name is a native American word originally referring to any nut that required a stone to crack it open.

SERVES 8 **PREPARATION TIME** 20 minutes (+ 30 minutes chilling) **COOKING TIME** 1 hour

1 quantity sweet shortcrust pastry (see pages 16–17)
40 g (1½ oz) butter, melted
110 g (3¾ oz/½ cup, firmly packed) dark brown sugar
175 g (6 oz/½ cup) golden syrup
1 teaspoon natural vanilla extract
2 eggs, lightly whisked
200 g (7 oz/2 cups) pecan halves
2 tablespoons apricot jam
Thick (double/heavy) or whipped cream, to serve

1 Preheat the oven to 200°C (400°F/Gas 6). Use a lightly floured rolling pin to roll out the pastry on a lightly floured work surface to a 30 cm (12 inch) diameter circle, taking care not to overwork the dough or it will become too soft. Roll the pastry around the rolling pin and ease it into a 3 cm (1¼ inch) deep, round 24 cm (9½ inch) fluted loose-based tart (flan) tin, pressing it into the base and side with your fingertips (see page 20). Roll the rolling pin over the tin to trim the excess pastry.

2 Line the pastry shell with non-stick baking paper and fill with baking beads, dried beans or uncooked rice. Bake for 20 minutes, then remove the paper and weights. Reduce the temperature to 160°C (315°F/Gas 2–3).

3 Meanwhile, put the butter, sugar, golden syrup, vanilla and egg in a bowl and whisk until well combined *(pic 1)*. Scatter the pecans evenly over the tart shell *(pic 2)*. Pour over the golden syrup mixture *(pic 3)*. Bake for 40 minutes or until the filling is browned and firm to touch. Place on a wire rack and cool the pie in the tin.

4 Put the jam in a small saucepan and heat until warm. Push through a sieve to remove any solids. Brush the sieved jam over the top of the pie to glaze. Serve at room temperature with the cream.

1

2

3

TIP Pecan pie will keep for 2–3 days in an airtight container. Like most cooked pastries, it should not be refrigerated if possible, as refrigeration spoils the texture of cooked pastry.

Pear and almond flan

SERVES 8 **PREPARATION TIME** 30 minutes (+ 2 hours 30 minutes chilling time) **COOKING TIME** 1 hour 10 minutes

PASTRY

150 g (5½ oz/1¼ cups) plain (all-purpose) flour

90 g (3¼ oz) unsalted butter, chilled and cubed

55 g (2 oz/¼ cup) caster (superfine) sugar

2 egg yolks, lightly beaten

FILLING

165 g (5¾ oz) unsalted butter, softened

150 g (5½ oz/⅔ cup) caster (superfine) sugar

3 eggs

125 g (4½ oz/1¼ cups) almond meal

1½ tablespoons plain (all-purpose) flour

2 firm, ripe pears

Icing (confectioners') sugar, to dust

1 Lightly grease a 24 cm (9½ inch) loose-based, fluted flan (tart) tin.

2 To make the pastry, sift the flour into a bowl. Using your fingertips, rub in the butter until the mixture resembles fine breadcrumbs. Stir in the sugar and mix together. Make a well in the centre, add the egg yolks and mix with a flat-bladed knife, using a cutting action, until the mixture comes together in beads. Turn out onto a lightly floured surface and gather into a ball. Wrap in plastic wrap and refrigerate for 30 minutes.

3 Preheat the oven to 180°C (350°F/Gas 4). Roll out the pastry between two sheets of baking paper until large enough to line the base and side of the tin. Line the tin with the pastry and trim the edge. Sparsely prick the base with a fork. Line the base with baking paper, evenly spread a layer of baking beads or uncooked rice over the paper and bake for 10 minutes. Remove the paper and beads and bake for a further 10 minutes. Cool.

4 To make the filling, beat the butter and sugar in a bowl using electric beaters for 30 seconds (don't cream the mixture). Add the eggs one at a time, beating after each addition. Fold in the almond meal and flour and spread the filling smoothly over the cooled pastry base.

5 Peel the pears, halve lengthways and remove the cores. Cut crossways into 3 mm (⅛ inch) slices. Separate the slices slightly, then place the slices on top of the tart to form a cross. Bake for about 50 minutes, or until the filling has set (the middle may still be a little soft).

6 Cool in the tin, then refrigerate for at least 2 hours before serving, dusted with icing sugar.

Rosemary & honey rice-custard tart

This tart is inspired by the flavours and ingredients of Italy, where rice is often used this way in desserts. A spoonful of lightly sweetened apple purée would make the perfect accompaniment, though the tart is wonderful served simply as is.

MAKES 26 cm (10½ inch) tart **PREPARATION TIME** 20 minutes (+ 60–75 minutes chilling) **COOKING TIME** 1 hour

- **1 quantity pâte sucrée (see page 19)**
- **1 tablespoon finely chopped rosemary, plus extra sprigs, to garnish**
- **110 g (3¾ oz/½ cup) short-grain white rice**
- **250 ml (9 fl oz/1 cup) milk**
- **300 ml (10½ fl oz) pouring (whipping) cream**
- **175 g (6 oz/½ cup) honey**
- **1 teaspoon natural vanilla extract**
- **1 egg**
- **2 egg yolks**

1 Make the pastry as directed, adding the rosemary to the flour. Use a rolling pin to roll out the chilled pastry on a lightly floured work surface to a 36 cm (14¼ inch) diameter circle and ease into a 2.5 cm (1 inch) deep, round 26 cm (10½ inch) fluted loose-based tart (flan) tin, using your fingertips to press it into the base and side of the tin (see page 20). Roll the rolling pin over the top of the tin to trim the excess pastry. Refrigerate for 30 minutes.

2 Preheat the oven to 180°C (350°F/Gas 4). Line the pastry shell with non-stick baking paper and fill with baking beads, dried beans or uncooked rice. Bake for 15 minutes, remove the paper and weights and bake for a further 6–7 minutes or until light golden and dry on the base *(pic 1)*. Transfer to a wire rack to cool slightly.

3 Meanwhile, combine the rice, milk and 125 ml (4 fl oz/½ cup) of the cream in a small saucepan and bring to a simmer over medium heat. Reduce the heat to low and cook, covered, for 18–20 minutes, stirring occasionally, or until the rice is nearly tender and the mixture is very thick. Remove from the heat, stir in the honey and vanilla and set aside to cool slightly *(pic 2)*.

4 Add the remaining cream, the egg and egg yolks and stir to combine well. Pour the mixture into the pastry shell *(pic 3)* and bake for 35 minutes or until the filling is just set. Transfer to a wire rack and cool in the tin. Serve the tart at room temperature, sprinkled with rosemary sprigs.

1

2

3

TIP This tart is best eaten on the day it is baked.

Small Pies & Tarts

Mini prawn and avacado tartlets

What's really special about these beautiful little tarts is that once you've cooked the pastry shells, the work is virtually done. The filling requires no cooking and can be put in place just before serving.

MAKES 48 **PREPARATION TIME** 35 minutes (+ 1 hour chilling, and cooling) **COOKING TIME** 15 minutes

1 quantity shortcrust pastry (see pages 16–17)
24 (about 400 g/14 oz) cooked medium prawns (shrimp), peeled and deveined
2–3 tablespoons lemon or lime juice
1 small (200 g/7 oz) avocado
200 g (7 oz) punnet small grape tomatoes, quartered
2 long red chillies, seeded and finely diced
48 coriander (cilantro) leaves

1 Preheat the oven to 180°C (350°F/Gas 4).

2 Cut the pastry into 2 equal portions. Use a rolling pin to roll out each portion between 2 sheets of non-stick baking paper until 2–3 mm (1/16–1/8 inch) thick. Refrigerate for 20 minutes to chill.

3 Remove one pastry portion from the refrigerator. Peel off the top sheet of paper. Use a round 5 cm (2 inch) pastry cutter to cut out 24 circles. Press each circle gently into a 1 cm (1/2 inch) deep, 4 cm (1 1/2 inch) diameter (base measurement) fluted tartlet tin *(pic 1)*. Roll the rolling pin gently over the tins to trim the excess pastry, then place the tins on a baking tray and refrigerate.

4 Repeat with the remaining portion of pastry to line another 24 tartlet tins. Refrigerate for 10 minutes or until all the pastry is well chilled.

5 Line each pastry shell with a small square of non-stick baking paper and fill with baking beads. Bake for 8 minutes. Remove the paper and beads and bake for a further 5–7 minutes or until the pastry is golden and crisp. Cool for 2 minutes in the tins, then transfer to a wire rack to cool completely.

6 Slice the prawns in half lengthways and place in a medium bowl *(pic 2)*. Drizzle with half the lemon juice and season with salt and freshly ground black pepper. Finely dice the avocado and place in a separate bowl with the tomatoes, chillies and remaining lemon juice. Season well with salt and pepper.

7 Spoon a teaspoonful of the avocado and tomato mixture into each pastry case *(pic 3)*. Top each with a prawn half and a coriander leaf. Serve immediately.

1

2

3

TIP The pastry shells can be made up to 2 days in advance. Keep in an airtight container.

Tomato & fennel tartlets with basil pesto

These mini quiches make excellent party or finger food. Any remaining basil pesto can be tossed through pasta with roasted cherry tomatoes or served with barbecued chicken or lamb.

MAKES 24 **PREPARATION TIME** 25 minutes (+ 15 minutes chilling) **COOKING TIME** 23 minutes

1 quantity parmesan shortcrust pastry (see page 17)
1 tablespoon olive oil
1 medium fennel bulb, trimmed, thinly sliced
75 g (2¾ oz/¾ cup, loosely packed) coarsely grated cheddar cheese
2 eggs
160 ml (5¼ fl oz/⅔ cup) pouring (whipping) cream
80 ml (2½ fl oz/⅓ cup) milk
12 cherry tomatoes, halved
Basil pesto
55 g (2 oz/2 cups, firmly packed) basil leaves
2 garlic cloves, coarsely chopped
40 g (1½ oz/¼ cup) toasted pine nuts
35 g (1¼ oz/⅓ cup) finely grated parmesan cheese
125 ml (4 fl oz/½ cup) olive oil

1 Grease two 12-hole (40 ml/1¼ fl oz/2 tablespoon) flat-based patty pan tins with oil or butter. Divide the pastry into 2 portions and roll out a portion on a lightly floured work surface to 3 mm (⅛ inch) thick. Use a round 6.5 cm (2½ inch) cutter to cut discs from the pastry. Press the pastry discs into the greased holes and prick all over with a fork. Repeat with the remaining pastry portion to line the remaining greased patty pans. Cover with plastic wrap and refrigerate for 15 minutes.

2 Preheat oven to 200°C (400°F/Gas 6).

3 Heat the oil in a large frying pan over medium–high heat. Add the fennel and cook, stirring, for 4–5 minutes or until light golden and soft *(pic 1)*. Divide the fennel and cheese evenly among the pastry shells.

4 Whisk the eggs, cream and milk in a small bowl until combined. Season well with salt and freshly ground black pepper. Transfer to a jug and divide evenly among the pastry shells. Top each with a cherry tomato half *(pic 2)*.

5 Bake the quiches for 18 minutes or until the filling is just set. Set aside for 5 minutes before removing from the trays.

6 Meanwhile, to make the basil pesto, blend or process the basil, garlic, pine nuts and parmesan in a food processor until almost smooth. With the motor running, gradually add the oil in a thin, steady stream, until thick and well combined *(pic 3)*. Season with salt and freshly ground black pepper.

7 Serve the quiches warm or at room temperature, topped with a little pesto.

1

2

3

TIP Keep in an airtight container in the refrigerator for up to 2 days. To reheat, return to the trays and put in a preheated 180°C (350°F/Gas 4) oven for 5–8 minutes.

Creamy snapper pies

SERVES 4 **PREPARATION TIME:** 25 minutes **COOKING TIME:** 1 hour 20 minutes

- **2 tablespoons olive oil**
- **4 onions, thinly sliced**
- **375 ml (13 fl oz/1½ cups) fish stock**
- **875 ml (30 fl oz/3½ cups) pouring (whipping) cream**
- **1 kg (2 lb 4 oz) skinless, boneless snapper fillets, cut into large pieces**
- **2 sheets puff pastry, thawed**
- **1 egg, lightly beaten**

1 Preheat the oven to 220°C (425°F/Gas 7). Heat the oil in a large deep-sided frying pan, add the onion and cook, stirring occasionally, over medium heat for 20 minutes, or until the onion is golden brown and slightly caramelised.

2 Add the stock, bring to the boil and cook for 10 minutes, or until the liquid has nearly evaporated. Stir in the cream and bring to the boil. Reduce the heat and simmer for about 20 minutes, until the liquid has reduced by half or until it coats the back of a spoon.

3 Divide half the sauce among four deep, 500 ml (17 fl oz/2 cup) ovenproof dishes. Put one-quarter of the fish pieces in each dish, then divide the remaining sauce among the dishes.

4 Cut the pastry sheets into shapes slightly larger than the tops of the dishes. Brush the edges of the pastry with a little of the egg. Press onto the dishes. Brush lightly with the remaining beaten egg. Bake for 30 minutes, or until the pastry is golden and puffed.

TIP: You can substitute bream, sea perch or garfish for the snapper.

Individual meat pies

MAKES 4 **PREPARATION TIME** 45 minutes (+ 30 minutes chilling) **COOKING TIME** 3 hours 5–10 minutess

2 tablespoons plain flour
600 g (1 lb 5 oz) chuck steak, cut into 1 cm (1/2 inch) pieces
60 ml (2 fl oz/1/4 cup) olive oil
4 brown onions, thinly sliced
1 medium carrot, finely chopped
1 celery stalk, finely chopped
2 garlic cloves, crushed
1 teaspoon caster (superfine) sugar
125 ml (4 fl oz/1/2 cup) red wine
500 ml (17 fl oz/2 cups) beef stock
200 g (7 oz) Swiss brown mushrooms, trimmed and quartered
1 quantity shortcrust pastry (see pages 16–17)
1 egg, lightly whisked

1 Place flour in a large bowl and season with sea salt and freshly ground black pepper. Add the beef, toss to coat in flour and shake off excess.

2 Heat 1 tablespoon of the oil in a large heavy-based flameproof casserole over medium–high heat. Add half the beef and cook, turning often, for 5 minutes or until browned all over. Transfer to a plate and repeat with the remaining beef, adding a little extra oil if necessary.

3 Heat half the remaining oil in the casserole. Add the onions, carrot and celery and cook over medium heat, stirring occasionally, for 10–12 minutes or until soft. Add the garlic and sugar and cook, stirring, for 30 seconds.

4 Add the wine and bring to boil. Reduce heat to low and simmer, uncovered, for 2 minutes or until slightly reduced. Return the beef to the casserole with the stock. Bring to boil, then reduce the heat and simmer, covered, for 1 hour. Uncover and cook for a further 1 hour or until the meat is very tender and the liquid has thickened.

5 Meanwhile, heat remaining oil in a frying pan over medium–high heat. Add mushrooms and cook, stirring, for about 5 minutes or until browned all over. Add to beef mixture and stir to combine. Transfer to a bowl and cool to room temperature.

6 Preheat oven to 180°C (350°F/Gas 4). Divide pastry into 2 portions, one twice as big as the other *(pic 1)*. Use a lightly floured rolling pin to roll out the smaller portion of pastry on a lightly floured work surface until 3 mm (1/8 inch) thick. Use the top of an 11 cm (4 1/4 inch) (top diameter), 7.5 cm (3 inch) (base diameter) pie tin to cut 4 rounds from the pastry *(pic 2)*.

7 Divide the larger portion of pastry into 4 equal portions and roll each out on a lightly floured work surface, taking care not to overwork the dough, into a 15 cm (6 inch) diameter round. Carefully ease each round into a pie tin, using fingertips to press them into base and side. Roll the rolling pin over the tops to trim excess pastry.

8 Divide the beef mixture among the pastry-lined tins *(pic 3)*. Brush the top edges of the pastry with egg. Place the smaller pastry rounds on top to cover beef mixture and use a lightly floured fork to press the edges together. Use a small sharp knife to make 2 slits in the top of each pastry lid. Brush tops lightly with egg and bake for 40 minutes or until golden. Set aside for 10 minutes, then remove from tins. Serve hot.

1

2

3

TIP These pies are best eaten on the day they are made. If you have more pies than you need, freeze them in sealed freezer bags for up to 2 months. Thaw overnight in the refrigerator and reheat in an oven preheated to 180°C (350°F/Gas 4) for 20–25 minutes.

Mango & passionfruit pies

MAKES about 6 **PREPARATION TIME** 1 hour 10 minutes (+ 60 minutes chilling time) **COOKING TIME** 25 minutes

400 g (14 oz/3¼ cups) plain (all-purpose) flour
165 g (5¾ oz/1⅓ cups) icing (confectioners') sugar
200 g (7 oz) cold unsalted butter, chopped
2 egg yolks, mixed with 2 tablespoons iced water
1 egg, lightly beaten
Icing (confectioners') sugar, for dusting
Whipped cream, to serve

FILLING
60 ml (2 fl oz/¼ cup) strained passionfruit pulp
1 tablespoon custard powder or instant vanilla pudding mix
3 ripe mangoes (900 g/2 lb), peeled, sliced and chopped
80 g (2¾ oz/⅓ cup) caster (superfine) sugar

1 Sift the flour and icing sugar into a large bowl. Using your fingertips, lightly rub in the butter until the mixture resembles coarse breadcrumbs. Make a well in the centre, then add the egg yolks to the well. Mix using a flat-bladed knife until a rough dough forms. Turn out onto a lightly floured work surface, then gently press together into a ball. Form into a flat disc, cover with plastic wrap and refrigerate for 30 minutes.

2 Grease six 10 x 8 x 3 cm (4 x 3¼ x 1¼ inch) fluted, loose-based flan (tart) tins or round pie dishes.

3 Roll out two-thirds of the chilled pastry between two sheets of baking paper until 3 mm (⅛ inch) thick. Cut out six bases to fit the prepared tins. Gently press them into the tins and trim the edges. Refrigerate for 30 minutes.

4 Meanwhile, preheat the oven to 190°C (375°F/Gas 5).

5 To make the filling, put the passionfruit pulp and custard powder in a small saucepan and mix together well.

6 Stir over medium heat for 2–3 minutes, or until the mixture has thickened. Remove from the heat, then stir in the mango and sugar.

7 Roll out the remaining pastry between two sheets of baking paper until 3 mm (⅛ inch) thick. Cut out six pie lids. Re-roll the pastry trimmings and cut into shapes for decoration.

8 Divide the filling among the pastry cases and brush the edges with beaten egg. Top with the pastry lids and press the edges to seal. Trim the edges and decorate the tops with the pastry shapes. Brush with beaten egg and dust with icing sugar.

9 Bake for 20–25 minutes, or until the pastry is golden. Remove from the oven and leave to cool in the tins.

10 Serve warm or at room temperature with whipped cream.

TIP Mango and passionfruit pies are best eaten the day they are made.

Individual berry tarts

MAKES 10 **PREPARATION TIME** 25 minutes (+ 1–1½ hours chilling and cooling) **COOKING TIME** 20 minutes

165 g (5¾ oz/½ cup) good-quality berry jam
250 g (9 oz) mascarpone cheese
125 ml (4 fl oz/½ cup) pouring (whipping) cream
2 tablespoons icing (confectioners') sugar, sifted, plus extra, to dust
½ vanilla bean, split lengthways and seeds scraped
350 g (12 oz) mixed fresh berries, such as raspberries, blackberries and blueberries

1 Make the pastry as directed, rolling it into a 10 cm (4 inch) long log before wrapping in plastic wrap and refrigerating for 30–60 minutes or until firm (see tip).

2 Cut the pastry log into 10 even discs *(pic 1)*. Place a disc between 2 sheets of non-stick baking paper and then use a rolling pin to roll out to about 12 cm (4½ inches) in diameter. Place the pastry round in a 6 cm (2½ inch) diameter (base measurement) tart (flan) tin with removable base and use your fingertips to press it gently into the base and side *(pic 2)*. Trim any overhanging pastry by rolling the rolling pin over the top of the tin. Place on a baking tray. Repeat with the remaining pastry discs to make 10 pastry shells in total. Refrigerate for 30 minutes.

3 Meanwhile, preheat the oven to 200°C (400°F/Gas 6).

4 Line the pastry shells with non-stick baking paper and fill with baking beads *(pic 3)*, dried beans or uncooked rice. Bake for 10 minutes, then remove the weights and paper. Bake for a further 8–10 minutes or until golden and cooked through. Remove from the oven and cool completely in the tins.

5 Divide the jam among the pastry shells and spread to coat the bases. Place the mascarpone, cream, icing sugar and vanilla seeds in a medium bowl. Use a balloon whisk to gently whisk until very soft peaks form, being careful not to overwork the mascarpone. Divide the mixture among the tart cases and top with the berries. Dust with extra icing sugar to serve.

VARIATION

Individual cherry tarts: Use good-quality cherry jam instead of the berry jam and use 650 g (1 lb 7 oz) cherries, pitted, instead of the mixed berries.Preheat the oven to 180°C (350°F/Gas 4). Line two baking trays with non-stick baking paper.

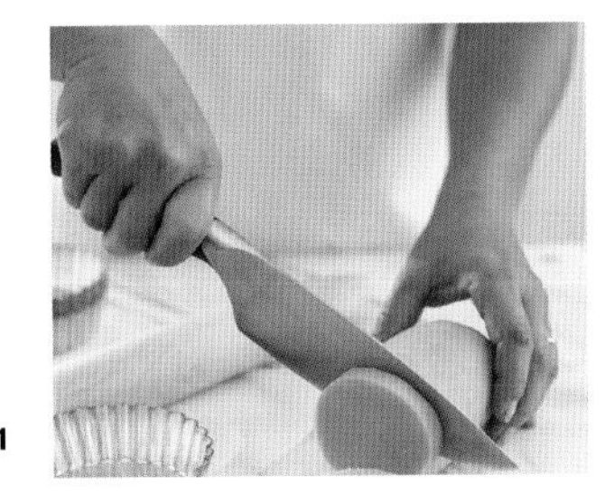
1

2

3

TIP Rolling the pastry into a log shape makes it easier to divide it into 10 equal portions. You can simply slice off discs that are then rolled into rounds just the right size for the tins.

Neenish tarts

MAKES 12 **PREPARATION TIME** 45 minutes (+ 30 minutes cooling) **COOKING TIME** 15 minutes

- 2 tablespoons plain (all-purpose) flour
- 70 g (2½ oz/⅔ cup) ground almonds
- 60 g (2¼ oz/½ cup) icing (confectioners') sugar, sifted
- 1 egg white, lightly beaten

CREAMY FILLING

- 1 tablespoon plain (all-purpose) flour
- 125 ml (4 fl oz/½ cup) milk
- 2 egg yolks
- 60 g (2¼ oz) unsalted butter, softened
- 2 tablespoons caster (superfine) sugar
- ¼ teaspoon natural vanilla extract

ICING

- 125 g (4½ oz/1 cup) icing (confectioners') sugar
- 2 tablespoons milk
- 1 tablespoon unsweetened cocoa powder

1 Lightly grease a 12-hole shallow patty pan or mini muffin tin. Sift the flour into a bowl and stir in the ground almonds and icing sugar. Make a well in the centre, add the beaten egg white and mix with a flat-bladed knife, using a cutting action, until the mixture comes together in beads and forms a stiff paste. Turn onto a lightly floured surface and gently gather into a ball. Wrap in plastic wrap and refrigerate for 30 minutes, to firm.

2 Preheat the oven to 190°C (375°F/Gas 5). Roll out the dough between two sheets of baking paper to 3 mm (⅛ inch) thick. Cut the pastry into 12 circles with a 7 cm (2¾ inch) fluted cutter. Press the pastry circles into the greased patty pan and prick evenly with a fork. Bake for 10 minutes, or until lightly golden.

3 To make the filling, stir the flour and milk in a saucepan until smooth, then stir over medium heat for 2 minutes, or until the mixture boils and thickens. Remove from the heat, then quickly stir in the egg yolks until smooth. Cover the surface with plastic wrap and set aside to cool. Using electric beaters, beat the butter, sugar and vanilla in a bowl until light and creamy. Gradually add the cooled egg mixture and beat until smooth. Spoon some of the mixture into each pastry shell and gently smooth the tops with the back of a spoon.

4 To make the icing (frosting), combine the icing sugar and milk in a heatproof bowl, place over a saucepan of simmering water, making sure the base of the bowl does not touch the water, and stir until smooth and glossy. Remove, transfer half the icing to a small bowl, add the cocoa and stir until smooth.

5 Using a small, flat-bladed knife, spread plain icing over half of each tart, starting from the centre and making a straight line with the icing, then pushing the icing out to the edge. Allow to set. Reheat the chocolate icing and ice the other half of each tart. Allow the icing to set completely before serving.

Portuguese tarts

These tarts are called pastéis de nata, or cream pastries, in their homeland of Portugal. They are notoriously difficult to make as the pastry requires a high temperature and the custard a low one, however this recipe for the home cook is achievable and gives an authentic result.

MAKES 12 **PREPARATION TIME** 1 hour 15 minutes (+ 1 hour 20 minutes chilling) **COOKING TIME** 20–25 minutes

165 g (5¾ oz/¾ cup) caster (superfine) sugar, plus 1 tablespoon, extra
250 ml (9 fl oz/1 cup) milk
50 g (1¾ oz/⅓ cup) plain (all-purpose) flour
1 vanilla bean, split lengthways and seeds scraped
1 x 10 cm (4 inch) strip lemon zest
4 egg yolks
185 ml (6 fl oz/¾ cup) pouring (whipping) cream
1 teaspoon ground cinnamon
½ quantity puff pastry **(see pages 24–25)**

1 Preheat the oven to 240°C (475°F/Gas 8). Position an oven shelf at the top of the oven. (Tarts need to be cooked at the top of the oven where it's hottest.) Lightly grease a 12-hole 80 ml (2½ fl oz/⅓ cup) muffin tin.

2 Combine the sugar and 125 ml (4 fl oz/½ cup) water in a small saucepan over low heat. Cook, stirring, until the sugar dissolves. Bring to a simmer over medium heat and simmer for 5–7 minutes or until the mixture reaches soft-ball stage (112°C/235°F) on a sugar thermometer. Remove from the heat and set aside.

3 Meanwhile, put 60 ml (2 fl oz/¼ cup) of the milk and the flour in a small bowl and stir until smooth. Place the remaining milk, vanilla seeds and pod, and lemon zest in a small saucepan. Bring to the boil, then remove from the heat. Add the flour mixture, stirring constantly until smooth. Add the egg yolks, stirring constantly until well combined. Stir in the cream until combined. Add the sugar syrup in a slow, steady stream, stirring constantly until combined. Transfer to a heatproof jug and set aside to cool slightly while you roll out the pastry.

4 Combine the extra sugar and cinnamon in a small bowl. Use a lightly floured rolling pin to roll out the pastry on a clean work surface to a 30 x 35 cm (12 x 14 inch) rectangle. With a long side facing you, sprinkle the pastry with the cinnamon mixture. Starting at the side closest to you, roll up the pastry tightly to form a 35 cm (14 inch) long log *(pic 1)*. Cut the log into 12 slices, about 3 cm (1¼ inches) wide *(pic 2)*.

5 Working with one slice at a time, place, cut side down, on a lightly floured work surface. Gently press with the heel of your hand to flatten slightly, then use a lightly floured rolling pin to roll out the pastry to form a 9 cm (3½ inch) round *(pic 3)*. Use a round 9 cm (3½ inch) pastry cutter to trim the edges as necessary. Gently press each round into a greased muffin hole, using your fingertips to carefully press them into the base and side of each hole. Divide the custard mixture among the pastry shells. Bake for 6–10 minutes or until the custard is firm to touch and beginning to brown in patches. Cool in the tin for 5 minutes, then transfer to a wire rack to cool completely.

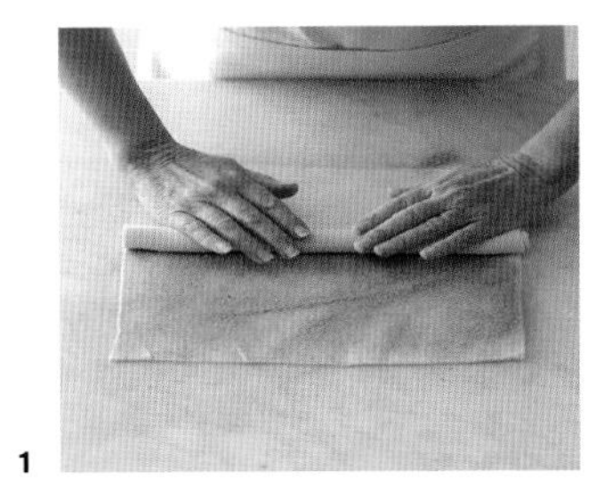

1

2

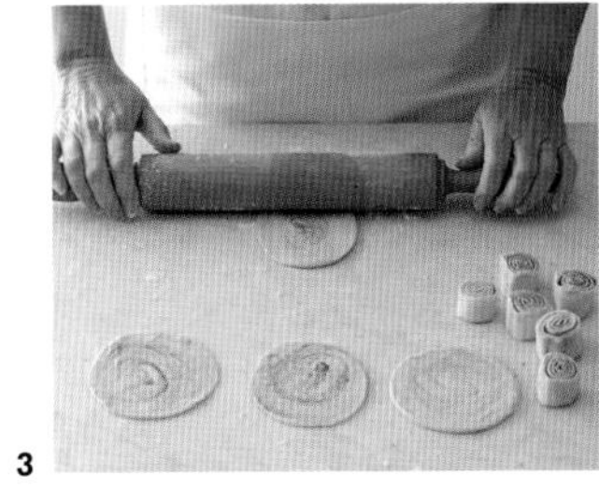

3

TIP These tarts are best eaten on the day they are baked.

Peach galettes

MAKES 12 **PREPARATION TIME** 1 hour 10 minutes (+ 60 minutes chilling time) **COOKING TIME** 30 minutes

- 400 g (14 oz/3¼ cups) plain (all-purpose) flour
- 165 g (5¾ oz/1⅓ cups) icing (confectioners') sugar, plus extra, for dusting
- 200 g (7 oz) cold unsalted butter, chopped
- 2 egg yolks, mixed with 2 tablespoons iced water

FILLING

- 600 g (1 lb 5 oz) firm, ripe peaches, stoned and thinly sliced
- 20 g (¾ oz) unsalted butter, melted
- 1 tablespoon honey
- 1 tablespoon caster (superfine) sugar
- ¼ teaspoon ground nutmeg
- 25 g (1 oz/¼ cup) flaked almonds, toasted

FOR GLAZING

- 1 egg yolk
- 1 tablespoon milk
- 80 g (2¾ oz/¼ cup) apricot jam

1 Sift the flour, icing sugar and a pinch of salt into a large bowl. Using your fingertips, lightly rub in the butter until the mixture resembles coarse breadcrumbs. Make a well in the centre, then add the egg yolks to the well. Mix using a flat-bladed knife until a rough dough forms. Turn out onto a lightly floured work surface, then gently press together into a ball. Form into a flat disc, cover with plastic wrap and refrigerate for 30 minutes.

2 Lightly grease a baking tray or line with baking paper. Roll out the pastry on a lightly floured work surface to 3 mm (⅛ inch) thick. Cut out twelve 12 cm (4½ inch) rounds.

3 To make the filling, put the peach slices, butter, honey, sugar and nutmeg in a bowl and gently toss together. Divide among the pastry rounds, leaving a 1 cm (½ inch) border around the edge. Fold the pastry over the filling, leaving the centre uncovered, and pleating the pastry edges at 1 cm (½ inch) intervals to fit. Place the galettes on the baking tray and refrigerate for 30 minutes.

4 Meanwhile, preheat the oven to 200°C (400°F/Gas 6).

5 To make the glaze, mix together the egg yolk and milk, then brush over the chilled pastry. Bake for 30 minutes, or until golden.

6 Meanwhile, put the jam and 1 tablespoon water in a small saucepan and stir over low heat until smooth.

7 Remove the galettes from the oven and brush the jam mixture over the hot galettes. Sprinkle with the almonds, then transfer to a wire rack to cool slightly. Serve warm or at room temperature, dusted with icing sugar.

TIP Peach galettes are best eaten the day they are made.

Christmas mince pies

Fruit mince can be made several months before Christmas and stored in an airtight container in the refrigerator. These sublime tarts are not hard to make and the work can be spread over a few days.

MAKES 12 **PREPARATION TIME** 1½ hours (+ 1 hour chilling and 8 hours soaking) **COOKING TIME** 2 hours 25 minutes

2 quantities sweet shortcrust pastry (see pages 16–17)
2 egg yolks, whisked with 1½ tablespoons water
Icing (confectioners') sugar, to dust

FRUIT MINCE
1 large granny smith apple, peeled, cored and finely chopped
65 g (2¼ oz/½ cup) suet mix (see tip)
120 g (4¼ oz/⅔ cup) raisins
85 g (3 oz/½ cup) sultanas (golden raisins)
75 g (2¾ oz/½ cup) currants
55 g (2 oz/⅓ cup) mixed peel (mixed candied citrus peel)
100 g (3½ oz/½ cup, lightly packed) dark brown sugar
Finely grated zest of 1 lemon
Finely grated zest of 1 small orange
2½ tablespoons lemon juice
2½ tablespoons orange juice
40 g (1½ oz/¼ cup) chopped blanched almonds
1 teaspoon ground cinnamon
¼ teaspoon ground nutmeg
Large pinch of ground cloves
80 ml (2½ fl oz/⅓ cup) brandy

1 To make the fruit mince (mincemeat), combine all the ingredients in a large heatproof bowl and toss to combine well *(pic 1)*. Cover with plastic wrap and set aside for 8 hours or overnight to soak.

2 Preheat the oven to 120°C (235°F/Gas ½). Remove the plastic wrap and cover the bowl with foil. Place in the oven and cook for 2 hours, stirring occasionally. Remove from the oven and set aside to cool *(pic 2)*.

3 Working with one quantity of pastry at a time, roll out on a lightly floured work surface until 5 mm (¼ inch) thick. Using a round 10 cm (4 inch) and a round 7.5 cm (3 inch) pastry cutter, cut out 12 rounds of pastry each. Gather the offcuts together and re-roll as required.

4 Use the large pastry rounds to line a 12-hole 80 ml (2½ fl oz/⅓ cup) muffin tin, pressing into the base and side with your fingertips. Divide the fruit mince among the pastry shells. Working with one small pastry round at a time, brush the edge lightly with the egg wash and place, egg side down, on a filled pastry shell, pressing the edges to join *(pic 3)*. Refrigerate for 30 minutes.

5 Meanwhile, preheat the oven to 180°C (350°F/Gas 4). Brush the tarts lightly with the egg wash and bake for 25 minutes or until the pastry is deep golden. Cool in the tin for 10 minutes, then carefully transfer to a wire rack to cool completely. Serve at room temperature, dusted with icing sugar.

1

2

3

TIP Suet is derived from the fat around beef kidneys. Suet mix is available from the baking section of the supermarket.

These tarts will keep, in an airtight container, for up to 10 days.

Baked custard tarts with rhubarb

MAKES 8 **PREPARATION TIME** 1 hour (+ 60 minutes chilling time) **COOKING TIME** 1 hour 20 minutes

400 g (14 oz/3¼ cups) plain (all-purpose) flour
½ teaspoon salt
165 g (53/4 oz/1⅓ cups) icing (confectioners') sugar
200 g (7 oz) cold unsalted butter, chopped
2 egg yolks, mixed with 125 ml (4 fl oz/½ cup) iced water

FILLING
½ vanilla bean, or ½ teaspoon natural vanilla extract
250 ml (9 fl oz/1 cup) milk
250 ml (9 fl oz/1 cup) pouring (whipping) cream
4 eggs
145 g (5 oz/⅔ cup) caster (superfine) sugar
400 g (14 oz/8 thin stalks) rhubarb, trimmed, then cut into 2 cm (¾ inch) lengths
95 g (3¼ oz/½ cup) soft brown sugar
½ teaspoon ground cinnamon
1 teaspoon lemon juice

1 Sift the flour, salt and icing sugar into a large bowl. Using your fingertips, lightly rub in the butter until the mixture resembles coarse breadcrumbs. Make a well in the centre, then add the egg yolks to the well. Mix using a flat-bladed knife until a rough dough forms. Turn out onto a lightly floured work surface, gently knead until smooth, then gently press together into a ball. Form into a flat disc, cover with plastic wrap and refrigerate for 30 minutes.

2 Lightly grease eight loose-based tartlet tins, measuring 10 cm (4 inches) in diameter and 3 cm (1¼ inches) deep.

3 Roll out the chilled pastry on a lightly floured work surface until 3 mm (⅛ inch) thick. Cut the pastry into eight rounds large enough to fit the base and side of the tartlet tins. Ease the pastry into the tins, pressing gently around the edges to fit. Trim the edges, then cover with plastic wrap and refrigerate for 30 minutes.

4 Meanwhile, preheat the oven to 200°C (400°F/Gas 6).

5 Prick the base of the chilled pastry cases with a fork. Line with baking paper and half-fill with baking beads, rice or dried beans. Bake for 15 minutes, then remove the paper and beads and bake for a further 7–8 minutes, or until the pastry is golden.

6 Remove the pastry from the oven and leave to cool. Reduce the oven temperature to 160°C (315°F/ Gas 2–3).

7 Meanwhile, make the filling. Split the vanilla bean down the middle and scrape the seeds into a saucepan (or put the vanilla extract in a saucepan). Add the milk and cream, then bring just to the boil. Whisk the eggs and caster sugar in a bowl until thick and pale. Whisk the milk mixture into the egg mixture, allow to cool a little, then strain into a bowl.

8 Pour the custard into the pastry cases and bake for 25–30 minutes, or until the filling has just set. Remove from the oven and increase the temperature to 180°C (350°F/Gas 4).

9 Put the rhubarb, sugar, cinnamon, lemon juice and 2 teaspoons water in a small baking dish, toss to combine, then cover with foil and bake for 30 minutes.

10 Remove the cooled tartlets from the tins and, just before serving, spoon the rhubarb and juices over the top. Serve warm or at room temperature.

TIP Baked custard tarts are best eaten the day they are made.

Pastries

Pork, apple & fennel sausage rolls

MAKES 12 **PREPARATION TIME** 1 hour (+ 1 hour 20 minutes chilling/cooling) **COOKING TIME** 35–40 minutes

1 tablespoon fennel seeds
1 tablespoon olive oil
1 small fennel bulb, trimmed and finely chopped
2 garlic cloves, finely chopped
60 g (2¼ oz/½ cup) chopped pancetta
Pinch of allspice
300 g (10½ oz) good-quality pork sausages, removed from their casings
300 g (10½ oz) minced (ground) pork
60 g (2¼ oz/1 cup, lightly packed) fresh breadcrumbs, made from day-old bread
1 small green apple (about 100 g/ 3½ oz), peeled and coarsely grated
¼ cup roughly chopped flat-leaf (Italian) parsley
1 egg yolk
1 quantity rough puff pastry (see pages 28–29)
1 egg, lightly whisked with
2 teaspoons water
1 tablespoon sesame seeds

1 Heat a small non-stick frying pan over medium heat. Add 3 teaspoons of the fennel seeds and cook, shaking the pan, for 30 seconds or until aromatic. Use a mortar and pestle or spice grinder to grind the seeds to a powder.

2 Heat the olive oil in a medium frying pan over medium–low heat. Add the chopped fennel and cook, stirring, for 5 minutes. Add the garlic and pancetta and cook for a further 5 minutes or until the fennel is golden and tender. Add the ground fennel and the allspice and cook for 30 seconds or until aromatic. Set aside to cool. Combine the sausage meat, minced pork, cooled fennel mixture, breadcrumbs, apple, parsley and egg yolk in a large bowl. Season well with salt and freshly ground black pepper.

3 Preheat the oven to 200°C (400°F/ Gas 6). Line 2 large baking trays with non-stick baking paper.

4 Cut the pastry in half widthways, then roll each piece out on a lightly floured work surface to a 25 cm (10 inch) square. Cut each pastry sheet in half. Divide the mince mixture into 4 equal portions. Shape each portion into a log and place on the centre of each piece of pastry (*pic 1*). Brush the edges of the pastry well with the egg wash. Fold the pastry over to enclose the filling, overlapping the edges and pressing to seal (*pic 2*). Transfer to a tray and refrigerate for 20 minutes to rest.

5 Line 2 more baking trays with non-stick baking paper. Place the sausage rolls on a chopping board, seam side down. Cut each roll into three equal pieces (*pic 3*). Transfer to the lined trays, allowing room for spreading.

6 Combine the remaining fennel seeds and the sesame seeds in a small bowl. Brush the sausage rolls with the egg wash and sprinkle with the seed mixture. Bake for 15 minutes, then reduce the temperature to 180°C (350°F/Gas 4), swap the trays around and cook for 10–15 minutes more or until puffed and golden.

1

2

3

TIP The uncooked sausage rolls can be frozen, in sealed freezer bags, for up to 2 months. There is no need to defrost them before cooking, but allow an extra 5 minutes to cook them through.

Potato and pea samosa

MAKES 16 **PREPARATION TIME** 1 hour 10 minutes (+ 1 hour resting/cooling) **COOKING TIME** 1 hour 15 minutes

- 500 g (1 lb 2 oz) all-purpose potatoes
- 120 ml (4 fl oz) vegetable oil, plus extra, for deep-frying
- 1 onion, finely chopped
- 110 g (3¾ oz/¾ cup) frozen peas, thawed and drained well
- 2 teaspoons finely grated ginger
- 2 garlic cloves, finely chopped
- 1 small green chilli, finely chopped
- 4 tablespoons finely chopped coriander (cilantro)
- 1 teaspoon salt
- 1 teaspoon ground cumin
- ¾ teaspoon ground coriander
- ¾ teaspoon garam masala
- 1½ tablespoons lemon juice
- 260 g (9¼ oz/1 cup) plain yoghurt
- 2 tablespoons finely chopped mint
- 225–260 g (8–9¼ oz/1½–1¾ cups) plain (all-purpose) flour
- 60 ml (2 fl oz/¼ cup) chilled water

1 Put the potatoes in a saucepan, cover with cold water and bring to the boil. Reduce the heat and simmer for 25–35 minutes or until tender. Drain the potatoes and allow to cool, then peel and cut into 1 cm (1/2 inch) pieces.

2 Heat 2 tablespoons of the oil in a large frying pan over medium–high heat. Cook the onion, stirring, for 6 minutes. Add the peas, ginger, garlic, chilli, half the chopped coriander and 2 tablespoons water. Reduce the heat to medium–low, cover and cook, stirring occasionally, for 3 minutes.

3 Reduce the heat to low, add the potatoes, half each of the salt and cumin, the ground coriander, garam masala and the lemon juice. Cook for 3–4 minutes, stirring occasionally. Transfer to a bowl.

4 Combine the yoghurt, remaining chopped coriander, remaining cumin and the mint. Refrigerate until required.

5 Sift 225 g (8 oz/1½ cups) of the flour and the remaining salt into a bowl. Add the remaining 80 ml (2½ fl oz/⅓ cup) oil and mix to combine. Gradually mix in the chilled water with a flat-bladed knife, using a cutting action, until a dough forms. Turn out and knead on a clean work surface for 5 minutes, adding the remaining flour, 1 tablespoon at a time, if it seems too wet. Shape into a ball and place in an oiled bowl, turning to coat in the oil. Cover with plastic wrap and set aside for 30 minutes.

6 Knead the pastry briefly, then divide into 8 equal portions. Roll each into a ball, place on a lightly greased baking tray and cover with plastic wrap. Working with one ball at a time, roll out to a 16 cm (6¼ inch) diameter circle, then cut in half. Pick up a semi-circle and dampen the straight side with a little water *(pic 1)*. Shape it into a cone, pinching the edges to seal. Spoon in 2 tablespoons of filling *(pic 2)*, then dampen the edges and pinch to seal, pleating slightly. Place on a lined tray. Repeat with remaining dough and filling.

7 Fill a small, deep saucepan one-third full with the extra oil and heat to 180°C (350°F). Fry the samosas, 3–4 at a time, for 6 minutes, turning once, or until golden and crisp. Drain on paper towels. Serve with the herbed yoghurt.

1

2

3

TIP If you like some chilli heat in your samosas, add ⅛ teaspoon chilli powder with the ground coriander and garam masala.

When in season, use fresh podded peas rather than frozen.

Spinach and feta triangles

MAKES 8 **PREPARATION TIME** 30 minutes **COOKING TIME** 45 minutes

1 kg (2 lb 4 oz) English spinach
80 ml (2½ fl oz/⅓ cup) olive oil
1 onion, chopped
10 spring onions (scallions), sliced
4 tablespoons chopped parsley
1 tablespoon chopped dill
large pinch of ground nutmeg
35 g (1¼ oz/⅓ cup) freshly grated parmesan cheese
150 g (5½ oz) crumbled feta cheese
90 g (3¼ oz) ricotta cheese
4 eggs, lightly beaten
40 g (1½ oz) butter, melted
12 sheets filo pastry

1 Trim any coarse stems from the spinach, then wash the leaves thoroughly, roughly chop and place in a large saucepan with just a little water clinging to them. Cover and cook over low heat for 5 minutes, or until wilted. Drain well and allow to cool slightly before squeezing tightly to remove the excess water.

2 Heat 60ml (2 fl oz/¼ cup) of the oil in a heavy-based frying pan. Add the onion and cook over low heat for 10 minutes, or until tender and golden. Add the spring onion and cook for another 3 minutes. Remove from the heat. Stir in the spinach, parsley, dill, nutmeg, parmesan, feta, ricotta and egg. Season well.

3 Preheat the oven to 180°C (350°F/ Gas 4). Lightly grease two baking trays. Combine the butter with the remaining oil. Work with three sheets of filo pastry at a time, keeping the rest covered with a damp tea towel (dish towel). Brush each sheet with butter mixture and layer them, then cut in half lengthways.

4 Place 4 tablespoons of the filling on an angle at the end of each strip. Fold the pastry over to enclose the filling and form a triangle. Continue folding the triangle over until you reach the end of the pastry. Put the triangles on the baking trays and brush with the remaining butter mixture. Repeat with the remaining filo and filling. Bake for 20–25 minutes, or until the pastry is golden brown.

1

2

TIP Feta is a traditional Greek-style salty cheese that should be stored in lightly salted water and kept refrigerated. Rinse and pat dry before using.

Chicken, bacon & mushroom vol-au-vents

MAKES 4 **PREPARATION TIME** 1 hour 20 minutes (+ 1 hour 35 minutes chilling) **COOKING TIME** 50–60 minutes

1 quantity puff pastry (see pages 24–25) (see tip)
1 egg, lightly whisked with 2 teaspoons water
225 g (8 oz) skinless chicken breast fillet
375 ml (13 fl oz/1½ cups) chicken stock
1 bay leaf
1 thyme sprig
1 tablespoon olive oil
75 g (2¾ oz) lean bacon, chopped
100 g (3½ oz) button mushrooms, sliced
2 small garlic cloves, crushed
1 French shallot, finely chopped
60 ml (2 fl oz/¼ cup) white wine
2 tablespoons cornflour (cornstarch), mixed with 60 ml (2 fl oz/¼ cup) water
60 ml (2 fl oz/¼ cup) pouring (whipping) cream
Thinly sliced spring onion (scallion), to garnish

1 Preheat the oven to 220°C (425°F/Gas 7). Line 2 baking trays with non-stick baking paper.

2 Use a rolling pin to roll out the pastry to a 36 cm (14¼ inch) square, then use a round 9 cm (3½ inch) pastry cutter to cut out 12 rounds. Place 4 rounds on a lined tray and use a round 6 cm (2½ inch) cutter to mark a small round in the centre of each, without cutting through. These are the bases.

3 Place the remaining pastry rounds on the other lined tray and use the smaller cutter to cut out the centre of each to make rings of an even thickness.

4 Brush the outer ring of each pastry base with egg wash, taking care not to brush the sides or the pastry won't rise properly. Carefully place a pastry ring on top of a pastry base. Brush the top of the ring with egg wash and place another ring on top. Repeat with the remaining bases, egg wash and rings. Refrigerate for 15 minutes or until well chilled. Brush the top ring of each pastry with egg wash, avoiding the sides.

5 Bake for 20 minutes or until puffed and golden. Remove any uncooked pastry from the centre and bake for 5–10 minutes or until the bases are golden and crisp. Cool on a wire rack.

6 Place the chicken and stock in a small saucepan. If the chicken isn't covered, add a little extra stock or water. Add the bay leaf and thyme and bring to a gentle simmer over medium heat. Reduce the heat to medium–low, cover and cook for 4–5 minutes. Remove from the heat and set aside for 10 minutes or until the chicken is just cooked through. Transfer the chicken to a plate and reserve the cooking liquid. Use 2 forks to shred the chicken and place in a medium bowl.

7 Heat the oil in a medium non-stick frying pan over medium–high heat. Add the bacon and cook, stirring, for 5 minutes. Add the mushrooms and garlic and cook, stirring, for a further 3 minutes. Add the shallot, season well and then mix into the chicken. Return the pan to the heat, add the wine and cook until reduced by half, then add the reserved cooking liquid. Bring to the boil, then reduce the heat and simmer for 2 minutes. Add the cornflour mixture and cream and stir until thickened. Remove the herbs. Add the chicken mixture and heat through. Season to taste. Spoon into the pastry cases and serve warm, sprinkled with spring onion.

TIP You can use 3 square 24 cm (9½ inch) sheets ready-made puff pastry or 4 large (8 cm/3¼ inch) ready-made vol-au-vent cases.

Unfilled vol-au-vents can be kept in an airtight container for up to 2 days. Before filling, heat in a preheated 180°C (350°F/Gas 4) for 5–7 minutes or until crisp.

Cornish pasties

This style of pasty was regular lunchtime fare for labourers working in the area around Cornwall in England during the 18th century. Today the Cornish pasty enjoys protected status under the European Commission, so only pasties made in Cornwall or to a traditional recipe can carry this name.

MAKES 8 **PREPARATION TIME** 1 hour (+ 30 minutes resting) **COOKING TIME** 45–50 minutes

PASTRY

600 g (1 lb 5 oz/4 cups) plain (all-purpose) flour
1 teaspoon salt
150 g (5½ oz) chilled butter, chopped
150 g (5½ oz) chilled lard (see tip), chopped
80 ml (2½ fl oz/⅓ cup) chilled water

FILLING

100 g (3½ oz) swede (rutabaga), peeled
100 g (3½ oz) potato, peeled
½ brown onion
350 g (12 oz) trimmed rump steak, cut into 8 mm (⅜ inch) pieces
1 tablespoon plain (all-purpose) flour
Milk, for brushing
1 egg yolk, whisked with 1½ tablespoons water

1 To make the pastry, combine the flour and salt in a large bowl. With your palms facing upwards, use your fingertips to rub in the butter and lard, lifting the flour mixture up as you rub to aerate it, until the mixture resembles fine breadcrumbs. Add almost all the chilled water and mix with a flat-bladed knife, using a cutting action, to form a dough, adding the remaining water if necessary. Knead briefly until the dough just comes together. Shape into a disc, wrap in plastic wrap and refrigerate for 30 minutes to rest.

2 Preheat the oven to 180°C (350°F/Gas 4) and line a large baking tray with non-stick baking paper. Cut the swede, potato and onion into 8 mm (⅜ inch) pieces. Combine it with meat in a large bowl. Scatter over the flour, season well with sea salt and freshly ground black pepper, then toss well.

3 Roll the pastry out on a lightly floured work surface until it is 5 mm (¼ inch) thick. Using a 16 cm (6¼ inch) plate or bowl as a guide, cut out 8 rounds from the pastry *(pic 1)*, gathering up the scraps and re-rolling as necessary. Brush the edges of the rounds lightly with milk, then divide the meat mixture among them, placing it along the centre and leaving a 1 cm (½ inch) border at each end *(pic 2)*.

4 Bring the sides of the pastry up to meet at the top, then press together. Crimp the edges together to seal well, using your fingers to push the edges into a decorative 'wave' *(pic 3)*. Place the pasties on the lined tray and brush all over with the egg wash. Bake for 45–50 minutes or until the pastry is deep golden. Cool slightly on the trays, then serve hot or at room temperature.

1

2

3

TIP Lard gives the pastry a beautiful, rich flaky quality but if it is hard to get, or you prefer, simply replace it with the equivalent weight in butter.

Raisin and custard spirals

These utterly delicious pastries use the same leavened pastry as croissants but are far easier to make as there is less precise measuring and cutting involved. They make an irresistible morning treat.

MAKES 10 **PREPARATION TIME** 1 1/2 hours (+ 4–4 1/2 hours proving and 1 1/2 hours chilling) **COOKING TIME** 33 minutes

1 quantity leavened puff pastry (see pages 30–31)
1/2 quantity crème pâtissière (see page 35), reducing the plain (all-purpose) flour to 1 tablespoon
1 egg yolk, whisked with 2 teaspoons water
130 g (4 1/2 oz/3/4 cup) raisins
115 g (4 oz/1/3 cup) apricot jam

1 Roll out the dough on a lightly floured work surface to a neat rectangle, about 28 x 60 cm (11 1/4 x 24 inches). Try to keep the edges as straight as possible.

2 With a short side facing you, use a large sharp knife to trim the edges so they are straight. Spread the cooled crème pâtissière over the dough *(pic 1)*, leaving a 1 cm (1/2 inch) border at the far end. Brush the border very lightly with the egg yolk mixture. Scatter the raisins evenly over the crème pâtissière.

3 Line 2 baking trays with non-stick baking paper. Starting at the short side facing you, roll the dough up into a short, thick log *(pic 2)*. Use a sharp serrated knife to cut the log in half widthways, then cut each portion into 5 slices, each about 2.5 cm (1 inch) wide *(pic 3)*. Place on the lined trays, cut-side down and allowing room for spreading. Set aside in a warm, draught-free place for 1 1/2 hours or until puffed and risen.

4 Preheat the oven to 200°C (400°F/Gas 6). Lightly brush the pastries all over with the egg yolk mixture. Bake for 30 minutes, swapping the trays halfway through to ensure even cooking, or until golden and crisp. Transfer to a wire rack to cool.

5 Combine jam and 1 tablespoon water in a small saucepan and bring to a simmer, stirring until smooth. Remove from heat and push through a sieve to remove any solids, then brush over the cooled pastries to glaze.

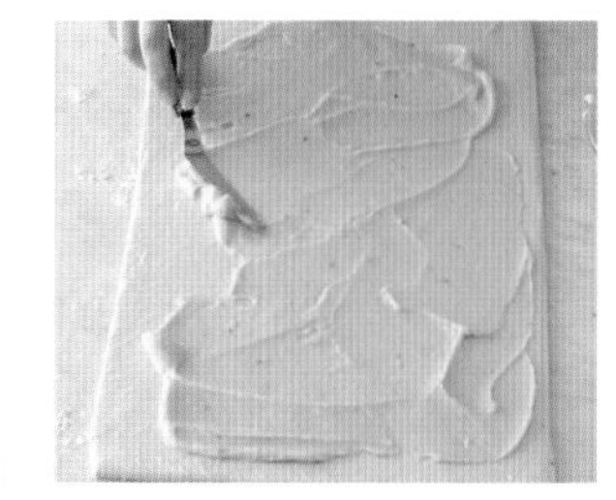
1

2

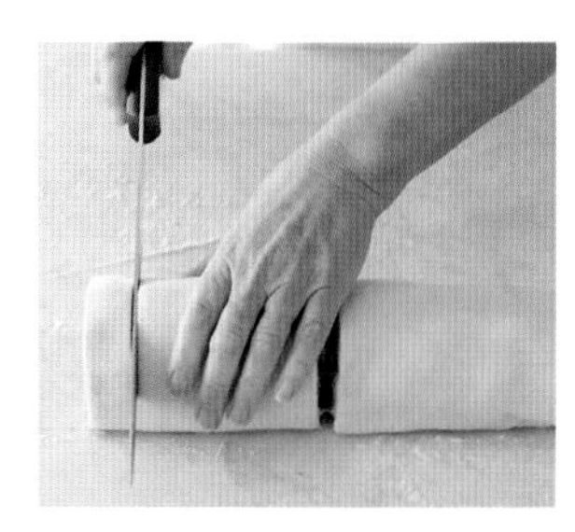
3

TIP These pastries are best eaten on the day they are baked.

Chocolate éclairs

One of the great classics of the French pastry repertoire, home-made éclairs never fail to impress. If you are short on time, simply fill them with sweetened whipped cream flavoured with vanilla.

MAKES 16 **PREPARATION TIME** 1½ hours (+ 40 minutes cooling/setting) **COOKING TIME** 44 minutes–1 hour

1 quantity choux pastry (see pages 32–33)
1 quantity crème pâtissière (see page 35), adding 1 tablespoon unsweetened cocoa powder when sifting the flour and cornflour
125 g (4½ oz) dark chocolate, melted

CHOCOLATE GLACÉ ICING
210 g (7½ oz/1¾ cups) icing (confectioners') sugar
15 g (½ oz) unsweetened cocoa powder
60–80 ml (2–2½ fl oz/¼–⅓ cup) boiling water
½ teaspoon natural vanilla extract

1 Preheat the oven to 200°C (400°F/Gas 6). Line 2 baking trays with non-stick baking paper. Spoon the pastry into a large piping (icing) bag fitted with a 1.5 cm (5⁄8 inch) plain nozzle (see page 42).

2 Pipe 10 cm (4 inch) lengths onto a lined tray, allowing room for spreading *(pic 1)*. Sprinkle the baking tray lightly with water to create steam in the oven and encourage the puffs to rise. Bake for 12–15 minutes. Reduce the heat to 180°C (350°F/Gas 4) and bake for a further 10–15 minutes, or until golden and puffed.

3 Transfer to a wire rack and use a small sharp knife to split each pastry in half to allow the steam to escape *(pic 2)*. Increase the temperature to 200°C (400°F/Gas 6) and pipe the remaining choux pastry into 10 cm (4 inch) lengths on the other lined tray. Cook the remaining pastries as before, then transfer to the wire rack and split in half. Allow to cool completely, then carefully remove any uncooked dough from inside each split pastry.

4 Make the crème pâtissière and while it is still warm, stir in the melted chocolate. Spoon the chocolate crème pâtissière into a large piping bag with a 1.5 cm (⅝ inch) plain nozzle. Pipe the crème onto the bottom half of the pastries *(pic 3)*, then cover with the tops of the pastries.

5 To make the chocolate glacé icing (frosting), sift the icing sugar and cocoa into a large bowl. Use a whisk to slowly stir in 60 ml (2 fl oz/¼ cup) of the boiling water to form a smooth icing with a light coating consistency. Stir in the vanilla. Add a little more water, a few drops at a time, if necessary, to reach the desired consistency. Spread about 1 tablespoon of icing over the top of each éclair. Set aside for 20 minutes or until the icing is set.

1

2

3

TIP Éclairs are best eaten as soon as possible after filling and icing. Keep refrigerated, but return to room temperature to serve.

Unfilled éclairs can be kept in an airtight container for up to 2 days or frozen in an airtight container for up to 2 weeks.

Baklava

This popular Middle Eastern treat consists of paper-thin filo pastry, buttered and layered with a nut and spice filling, then covered with a sweet syrup. Filo pastry is available fresh or frozen from supermarkets. Fresh filo is easier to work with, less fragile and won't tear as much as the frozen variety.

MAKES about 18 pieces **PREPARATION TIME** 30 minutes (+ cooling) **COOKING TIME** 30 minutes

400 g (14 oz/3½ cups) walnut halves, finely chopped
155 g (5½ oz/1 cup) almonds, finely chopped
½ teaspoon ground cinnamon
½ teaspoon mixed (pumpkin pie) spice
1 tablespoon caster (superfine) sugar
16 sheets filo pastry
200 g (7 oz) butter, melted
1 tablespoon olive oil

SYRUP
440 g (15½ oz/2 cups) sugar
330 ml (11¼ fl oz/1⅓ cups) water
3 whole cloves
3 teaspoons lemon juice

1 Preheat the oven to 180°C (350°F/Gas 4). Brush the base and sides of a shallow 18 x 28 cm (7 x 11¼ inch) tin with melted butter to grease.

2 Put the walnuts, almonds, spices and sugar in a medium bowl and mix well. Lay the filo pastry flat on a work surface and cover with a clean tea towel (dish towel), then a slightly damp tea towel to prevent it drying out. Combine the butter and oil.

3 Take 1 sheet of pastry and place it flat on the work surface. Brush liberally with the butter mixture, then fold it in half crossways. Trim the edges to fit the greased tin and then place in the tin. Repeat with 3 more pastry sheets to cover the base, brushing liberally with the butter mixture and trimming edges as needed *(pic 1)*.

4 Sprinkle one-third of the nut mixture over the pastry in the tin *(pic 2)*. Repeat this process to make 2 more layers each of pastry and nut mixture, then finish with another pastry layer. Press the top down with your hands so that the pastry and nuts stick to each other.

5 Brush the top of the pastry with the remaining butter and oil mixture. Use a large sharp knife to cut the baklava lengthways into 4 even strips, then diagonally into diamonds. Bake the baklava for 30 minutes or until the pastry is golden and crisp.

6 Meanwhile, to make the syrup, combine all the ingredients in a small saucepan and stir over low heat until the sugar dissolves. Bring to the boil, then reduce the heat and simmer, without stirring, for 10 minutes. Set aside to cool. Discard the cloves.

7 Pour the cooled syrup over the hot baklava *(pic 3)*, transfer to a wire rack and allow to cool in the tin. Cut into diamonds to serve.

1

2

3

TIP Keep in an airtight container, layered with non-stick baking paper, for up to 5 days.

Eccles cakes

These little pastries take their name from the English town of Eccles, where they originated. They are similar to the Chorley cake, also named after an English town, though they are made using flaky pastry rather than shortcrust. Both these pastries are traditionally served with Lancashire cheese.

MAKES 12 **PREPARATION TIME** 1 hour (+ 1½ hours chilling) **COOKING TIME** 25–30 minutes

1 quantity flaky pastry (see pages 26–27)
1 egg white, whisked
Caster (superfine) sugar, to sprinkle

FILLING
20 g (¾ oz) unsalted butter
60 g (2¼ oz/⅓ cup, lightly packed) dark brown sugar
115 g (4 oz/¾ cup) currants
40 g (1½ oz/¼ cup) mixed peel (mixed candied citrus peel)
1 teaspoon finely grated lemon zest
2 teaspoons lemon juice
¾ teaspoon mixed (pumpkin pie) spice

1 To make the filling, put the butter and sugar in a small saucepan over low heat and cook, stirring, for 2–3 minutes or until the butter melts and the mixture is smooth. Transfer to a bowl, add the remaining ingredients and stir to mix well. Set aside to cool.

2 Line 2 baking trays with non-stick baking paper. Roll out the pastry on a lightly floured work surface to a rectangle, about 32 x 42 cm (12¾ x 16½ inches) and 4 mm (¼ inch) thick. Use a round 10 cm (4 inch) pastry cutter to cut out 12 rounds. Place on the lined trays and refrigerate for 20 minutes.

3 Preheat the oven to 200°C (400°F/Gas 6).

4 Divide the filling among the rounds on the trays, placing it in a heap in the centre of each and leaving a border of about 1 cm (½ inch) *(pic 1)*. Working with one at a time, bring the edges up and over to fully enclose the filling and form a ball, pressing the edges to seal *(pic 2)*. Use your hand to press down on the pastry balls to flatten them *(pic 3)*. Turn them over — the filling should start showing through the pastry.

5 Brush the pastries with the egg white and sprinkle with the sugar. Use a small sharp knife to cut three small slits in the top of each pastry. Bake the pastries for 20–25 minutes or until deep golden. Transfer to a wire rack to cool.

1

2

3

TIP Eccles cakes will keep, stored in an airtight container, for up to 5 days.

ACIER EXTRA
GML
PARIS

Croissants

MAKES 10 **PREPARATION TIME** 1 hour 20 minutes (+ 3½–4½ hours proving and 1½ hours chilling)
COOKING TIME 17–22 minutes

1 quantity leavened puff pastry (see pages 30–31)
2 egg yolks, whisked with 1½ tablespoons water

1 Use a rolling pin to roll out the pastry on a lightly floured work surface to a neat 35 x 53 cm (14 x 21 inch) rectangle, keeping the edges as straight as possible and rotating the pastry often so you are always rolling away from yourself.

2 Use a large sharp knife to trim the edges so they are straight, forming a 32 x 48 cm (12¾ x 19 inch) rectangle, discarding the offcuts. Cut the pastry in half lengthways, making the cut as straight as possible. Don't separate the two strips. Measure and mark 16 cm (6¼ inch) intervals along either side of the cut down the centre of the pastry *(pic 1)*. On the two outside edges, measure and mark the first 8 cm (3¼ inches), then mark 16 cm (6¼ inch) intervals the rest of the way along. Make straight, diagonal cuts into the pastry to join the marks on each strip and form triangles *(pic 2)*.

3 Separate each pastry triangle, then elongate each one slightly by giving it a brief roll lengthways with a rolling pin. Working with one triangle at a time, place the short side nearest you and gently stretch the two ends to lengthen slightly. Make a 5 mm (¼ inch) cut into the base of each triangle, at the centre.

4 Roll the croissant up by rolling the base towards the tip *(pic 3)*. Turn the roll so the tip of the triangle is facing you, then bend to form a crescent shape.

5 Place on lined baking trays, cover with tea towels (dish towels) and set aside in a warm, draught-free place for 1–1½ hours or until puffed and risen. The croissants will not double in size.

6 Preheat the oven to 220°C (425°F/Gas 7). Brush the croissants all over with the egg wash. Bake for 2 minutes, then reduce the heat to 180°C (350°F/Gas 4). Bake for a further 15–20 minutes or until golden and puffed. Transfer to a wire rack. Serve warm or allow to cool.

VARIATION

Chocolate croissants: Roll the pastry out to a 34 x 50 cm (13½ x 20 inch) rectangle, then trim the edges to give a neat 32 x 48 cm (12¾ x 19 inch) rectangle. Cut the pastry in half lengthways, then neatly cut each strip into 6 rectangles, 8 cm (3¼ inches) wide. Coarsely chop 150 g (5½ oz) dark chocolate. Working with one rectangle at a time, place on a work surface with a short side facing you. Place a row of chopped chocolate along the end, then roll the bottom edge over to enclose. Make another row of chocolate and roll again to enclose, then roll up completely. Continue from step 5.

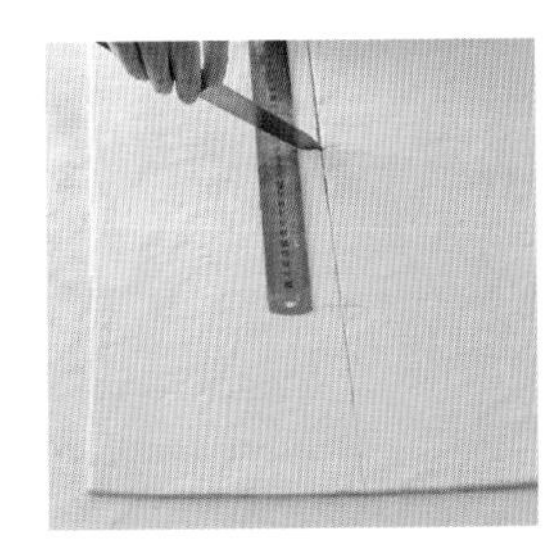

1

2

3

TIP Croissants are best eaten on the day they are baked but they can be frozen, in an airtight container or in sealed freezer bags, for up to 6 weeks. Reheat in the oven before serving.

Apple turnovers

Crisp puff pastry enclosing a sweet fruit filling with a hint of spice is a wonderful combination. You can experiment with other fruit fillings, such as cooked pears, plums, cherries or apricots. Just make sure you simmer or drain away any excess liquid or the pastry may burst and/or become soggy.

MAKES 6 **PREPARATION TIME** 1 hour (+ 1 hour 50 minutes chilling, and cooling) **COOKING TIME** 35 minutes

1 quantity puff pastry (see pages 24–25)
1 egg yolk, whisked with 1½ tablespoons water
55 g (2 oz/¼ cup) coffee crystals or raw (demerara) sugar

FILLING
3 large granny smith apples, peeled and cut into small pieces
130 g (4½ oz/¾ cup) raisins
75 g (2¾ oz/⅓ cup) caster (superfine) sugar
1 teaspoon ground cinnamon

1 To make the filling, put all the ingredients in a saucepan and add 60 ml (2 fl oz/¼ cup) water. Cover the pan tightly and cook over medium heat for 8–10 minutes or until the apple is soft. Remove the lid and cook for a further 3–4 minutes or until the excess liquid has evaporated. Remove from the heat and set aside to cool.

2 Use a rolling pin to roll out the pastry on a lightly floured work surface to a rectangle, about 24 x 36 cm (9½ x 14¼ inches). Use a lightly floured round 12 cm (4½ inch) pastry cutter or saucer of the same size to cut out 6 rounds. Working with one round at a time, roll out to an oval, about 20 cm (8 inches) long and 12 cm (4½ inches) wide *(pic 1)*, taking care not to stretch the dough or the pastry will shrink. Transfer to a tray and refrigerate for 30 minutes.

3 Preheat the oven to 200°C (400°F/Gas 6). Working with one oval at a time, brush the edges lightly with the egg wash. Divide the filling among the ovals, placing it over half of each oval and leaving a 1 cm (½ inch) border *(pic 2)*. Fold the uncovered pastry over the filling, pressing the edges together gently to seal. Do not crimp or fold, as this will prevent the pastry puffing up properly around the edges. Brush each pastry with egg wash and sprinkle with the coffee crystals. Make two small slashes on top of each pastry using the tip of a small sharp knife *(pic 3)*, then transfer to a lightly greased tray. Bake for 20 minutes or until puffed and golden. Transfer to a wire rack to cool to room temperature.

1

2

3

TIP Turnovers are best eaten on the day they are baked.

Danish pastries

MAKES 12 **PREPARATION TIME** 1 hour (+ 1 hour 30 minutes proving and 4 hours chilling) **COOKING TIME** 25 minutes

2 teaspoons dried yeast
125 ml (4 fl oz/1/2 cup) warm milk
1 teaspoon caster (superfine) sugar
250 g (9 oz/2 cups) plain (all-purpose) flour
55 g (2 oz/1/4 cup) caster (superfine) sugar, extra
1 egg, lightly beaten
1 teaspoon natural vanilla extract
250 g (9 oz) unsalted butter, chilled
40 g (1 1/2 oz) flaked almonds
80 g (2 3/4 oz/1/4 cup) apricot jam, to glaze

PASTRY CREAM
2 tablespoons caster (superfine) sugar
2 egg yolks
2 teaspoons plain (all-purpose) flour
2 teaspoons cornflour (cornstarch)
125 ml (4 fl oz/1/2 cup) hot milk

1 Stir the yeast, milk and sugar in a small bowl until dissolved. Leave in a warm, draught-free place for 10 minutes, or until bubbles appear on the surface. The mixture should be frothy and slightly increased in volume. If your yeast doesn't foam, it is dead, so discard it and start again. Sift the flour and 1/2 teaspoon salt into a large bowl and stir in the extra sugar. Make a well in the centre and add the yeast, egg and vanilla. Mix to a firm dough. Turn out onto a lightly floured surface and knead for 10 minutes to form a smooth, elastic dough. Place in a lightly greased bowl, cover and set aside in a warm place for 1 hour, or until doubled in size. Cut the butter in half lengthways and place between two sheets of baking paper. Use a rolling pin to pat out to a 15 x 20 cm (6 x 8 inch) rectangle and refrigerate.

2 Knock back the dough (one punch with your fist) and knead for 1 minute. Roll the dough out to a rectangle measuring 25 x 30 cm (10 x 12 inches). Put the butter in the centre of the dough and fold up the bottom and top of the dough over the butter to join in the centre. Seal the edges with a rolling pin. Give the dough a quarter-turn clockwise, then roll out to a 20 x 45 cm (8 x 17 3/4 inch) rectangle. Fold over the top third of the pastry, then the bottom third and then give another quarter-turn clockwise. Cover and refrigerate for 30 minutes. Repeat the rolling, folding, turning and chilling four more times. Wrap in plastic wrap and chill for at least another 2 hours.

3 To make the pastry cream, put the sugar, egg yolks and flours in a saucepan and whisk to combine. Pour the hot milk over the top and whisk until smooth. Bring to the boil over medium heat, stirring constantly, until the mixture boils and thickens. Cover and set aside.

4 Preheat the oven to 200°C (400°F/Gas 6) and line two baking trays with baking paper. On a lightly floured surface, roll the dough into a rectangle or square 3 mm (1/8 inch) thick. Cut the dough into 10 cm (4 inch) squares and place on the baking trays. Spoon 1 tablespoon of pastry cream into the centre of each square and top with two apricot halves. Brush one corner with the beaten egg and draw up that corner and the diagonally opposite one to touch in the middle between the apricots. Press firmly in the centre. Repeat with the remaining squares. Leave in a warm place to prove for 30 minutes. Brush each pastry with egg and sprinkle with almonds. Bake for 15–20 minutes, or until golden. Cool on wire racks. Melt the apricot jam with 1 tablespoon water in a saucepan and then strain. Brush the tops of the apricots with the hot glaze and serve.

Walnut, cinnamon & brown sugar palmiers

MAKES 12 **PREPARATION TIME** 20 minutes **COOKING TIME** 20–25 minutes

150 g (5½ oz/⅔ cup, firmly packed) light brown sugar
85 g (3 oz/⅔ cup) chopped walnuts
1½ teaspoons ground cinnamon
1 egg
1 egg yolk
3 sheets (25 x 25 cm/10 x 10 inch) frozen butter puff pastry, thawed

1 Preheat the oven to 200°C (400°F/Gas 6). Line 2 baking trays with non-stick baking paper. Combine the sugar, walnuts and cinnamon in a bowl.

2 Whisk together the egg and yolk in a small bowl until well combined. Place a piece of non-stick baking paper on your work surface. Put a pastry sheet on top and brush with a little of the whisked egg. Scatter evenly with a third of the sugar mixture. Brush another pastry sheet with a little egg and then place, brushed side down, over the first pastry sheet to cover the sugar mixture. Brush the top of the pastry with a little more egg, then scatter over half the remaining sugar mixture *(pic 1)*. Repeat with the remaining pastry sheet, egg and sugar mixture to make 1 more layer. Use your fingers to press down on the pastry so the layers stick together a little.

3 Starting with the pastry edge nearest you, roll the pastry up tightly (like a Swiss roll/jelly roll) until it reaches halfway across. Roll the opposite side of the pastry up tightly so they meet in the middle *(pic 2)*. Use a sharp knife to cut the log into 12 even slices. Working with one slice at a time, place between two sheets of non-stick baking paper and roll with a rolling pin to flatten to about 6 mm (¼ inch) and enlarge *(pic 3)*. Transfer to the lined trays.

4 Bake the palmiers for 20–25 minutes, swapping the trays around halfway through cooking, until they are deep golden and crisp.

VARIATION

Rosemary, sugar and clove twists: Replace the sugar, walnuts and cinnamon with 30 g (1 oz/½ cup) coffee crystals (or other very coarse sugar), 1½ tablespoons chopped rosemary leaves and ¼ teaspoon ground cloves. Reduce the pastry to 2 sheets and layer as before, scattering half the rosemary mixture between the sheets and half on top. Press down firmly with your fingers so the pastry sticks together. Instead of rolling the pastry, use a large sharp knife to cut it into 12 even strips. Carefully twist each strip several times, then place on the lined trays. Bake for 20 minutes, swapping trays as before, or until the pastry is deep golden and crisp.

1

2

3

TIP Palmiers are best eaten on the day of making but will keep in an airtight container for up to 2 days.

Honey & nut filo rolls

These mouthwatering morsels have all the exotic flavours of the Middle East, including cinnamon, honey and pistachio nuts. In that part of the world, it is usual for pastries, many of which are made using filo pastry, to be doused in a rich, sweet syrup.

MAKES 48 **PREPARATION TIME** 50 minutes (+ cooling) **COOKING TIME** 15–20 minutes

140 g (5 oz/1 cup) pistachios
140 g (5 oz/1 cup) walnut pieces
1 teaspoon ground cinnamon
55 g (2 oz/¼ cup) caster (superfine) sugar
150 g (5½ oz) unsalted butter, chopped
1½ tablespoons vegetable oil
16 sheets filo pastry (each measuring 27.5 x 43 cm/11 x 17 inches)
30 g (1 oz/¼ cup) pistachios, extra, finely chopped

SYRUP
350 g (12 oz/1 cup) honey
330 g (11½ oz/1½ cups) caster (superfine) sugar
10 whole cloves

1 Preheat the oven to 180°C (350°F/Gas 4). Line 2 baking trays with non-stick baking paper. Place the pistachios, walnuts, cinnamon and sugar in the bowl of a food processor and pulse until coarsely ground.

2 Heat the butter in a small saucepan over low heat until just melted. Add the oil and set aside. Lay the filo pastry flat on a work surface and cover with a clean tea towel (dish towel), then a slightly damp tea towel to prevent it drying out. Take 1 sheet of pastry and place it flat on the work surface. Brush with a little of the butter mixture, then top with another sheet of filo *(pic 1)*. Repeat with 2 more sheets of filo, brushing each sheet with the butter mixture. Sprinkle over 70 g (2½ oz/½ cup) of the nut mix.

3 Cut the pastry stack in half lengthways, then cut each strip into 6 evenly sized rectangles. Working with one rectangle at a time and starting with a shorter edge, roll up tightly into a cigar shape *(pic 2)*. Place on baking trays lined with non-stick baking paper. Brush with a little more butter mixture. Repeat with the remaining filo pastry, nut mix and butter mixture. Bake for 15–20 minutes or until golden.

4 Meanwhile, to make the syrup, combine all the ingredients in a saucepan over medium heat and stir until the sugar dissolves. Boil for 5 minutes, then remove from the heat.

5 Cool the filo rolls on the trays for 5 minutes, then transfer to a large tray. Drizzle two-thirds of the syrup over the warm filo rolls *(pic 3)*, then allow them to cool to room temperature.

6 To serve, arrange the filo rolls on a serving platter, drizzle with the remaining syrup and sprinkle with the extra pistachios.

1

2

3

TIP This recipe can be halved successfully, if desired.

The filo rolls will keep, covered with plastic wrap or in an airtight container, at room temperature for up to 3 days; do not refrigerate.

Lemon beignets

A beignet, which means 'fritter' in French, is a fried and sugared pastry that is not dissimilar to a doughnut, only without the hole in the centre. The recipe is very versatile, so try replacing the lemon zest with orange zest or adding raisins, currants or chopped candied peel if you like.

MAKES 24 **PREPARATION TIME** 30 minutes **COOKING TIME** 16–20 minutes

1 quantity choux pastry (see pages 32–33), increasing the sugar to 2 tablespoons
2 tablespoons finely grated lemon zest
1.25 litres (44 fl oz/5 cups) vegetable oil, for deep frying
Caster (superfine) sugar, to dredge

1 Make the choux pastry according to the recipe, beating in the lemon zest with the final addition of egg.

2 Heat the oil in a medium saucepan until it reaches 180°C (350°F) or until a cube of bread dropped into the oil turns golden brown in 15 seconds. Take a heaped teaspoon of the batter and use another teaspoon to push it into the oil *(pic 1)*. Cook 5–8 beignets at a time so you don't crowd the pan (this will depend on the size of your pan). Cook for 4 minutes, turning halfway through cooking, or until deep golden and cooked through. Use a slotted spoon to remove the beignets from the oil *(pic 2)*, drain well and transfer to a plate lined with paper towels. Repeat to cook the remaining batter.

3 Dredge the hot beignets in sugar to coat well *(pic 3)* and serve warm.

1

2

3

TIP Beignets are best eaten on the day they are baked.

Paris brest

This delicious choux pastry cake was created in 1891 by a French pastry chef to commemorate the Paris–Brest–Paris bicycle race. It was made in a ring shape to represent a wheel.

MAKES 1 cake **PREPARATION TIME** 1 hour 20 minutes (+ chilling) **COOKING TIME** 45 minutes

1 quantity choux pastry (see pages 32–33)
80 g (2¾ oz/¾ cup) flaked almonds
1½ quantities crème pâtissière (see page 35)
185 ml (6 fl oz/¾ cups) pouring (whipping) cream, whipped to firm peaks
165 g (5¾ oz/¾ cup) caster (superfine) sugar
Icing (confectioners') sugar, to dust

1 Preheat the oven to 200°C (400°F/Gas 6). Line a large baking tray with non-stick baking paper, mark a 22 cm (8½ inch) diameter circle and then turn the paper upside down.

2 Spoon the choux pastry into a large piping (icing) bag fitted with a 1 cm (½ inch) plain nozzle (see page 42). Pipe the dough onto the baking paper, following the circle, to make a ring with a thickness of about 2.5 cm (1 inch) *(pic 1)*. Pipe another circle of dough around the inside, leaving a 3 mm (⅛ inch) gap to allow for spreading *(pic 2)*. Pipe a third circle over the gap between the 2 rings, then use your fingers to very lightly smooth the surface slightly *(pic 3)*.

3 Scatter 25 g (1 oz/¼ cup) of the flaked almonds over the pastry, then bake for 25 minutes or until the pastry is golden and puffed. Transfer to a wire rack to cool completely.

4 Meanwhile, refrigerate the crème pâtissière until completely chilled. Fold through the whipped cream and refrigerate again until firm.

5 Line another baking tray with non-stick baking paper. Combine the sugar and 60 ml (2 fl oz/¼ cup) water in a saucepan over low heat. Cook, stirring, for 5 minutes or until the sugar dissolves. Increase the heat to high and bring to the boil. Boil, without stirring, for 5–7 minutes, regularly brushing down the side of the pan with a pastry brush dipped in water to avoid crystallisation. When the mixture is deep golden, remove from the heat and add the remaining almonds. Pour immediately onto the lined tray and set aside to cool and harden. Break up into small pieces, then process in a food processor to a fine powder. Stir into the chilled crème pâtissière.

6 Use a sharp serrated knife to slice the Paris Brest in half horizontally. Remove any uncooked dough. Place the bottom half on a serving plate or platter. Spoon the crème pâtissière into a large piping (icing) bag fitted with a 1 cm (½ inch) plain nozzle. Pipe the filling onto the base. Top with the remaining pastry ring and dust with the icing sugar.

1

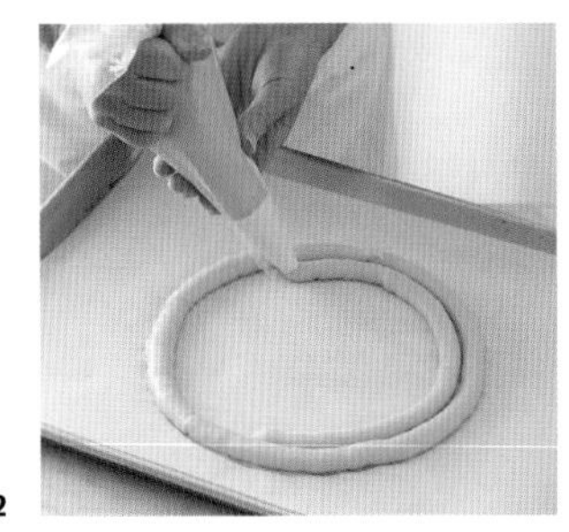

2

3

TIP Paris brest is best eaten on the day it is made, as the praline quickly melts and loses its texture.

If you would like a garnish, sliced fresh strawberries are a wonderful accompaniment.

Cream cheese and cherry strudel

This is a cheat's version of a strudel, the filled and rolled pastry creation from Austria. Ready-made filo pastry is used instead of the traditional home-made stretched, thin dough, but it gives a similar result.

SERVES 6 **PREPARATION TIME** 40 minutes (+ cooling) **COOKING TIME** 1 hour

2 x 415 g (14¾ oz) tins pitted black cherries in syrup
250 g (9 oz) cream cheese
110 g (3¾ oz/½ cup) caster (superfine) sugar
1 teaspoon natural vanilla extract
1 egg
1 egg yolk
2 tablespoons plain (all-purpose) flour
125 g (4½ oz) butter, melted
8 sheets filo pastry (see tip), at room temperature
70 g (2½ oz/⅔ cup) almond meal
35 g (1¼ oz/⅓ cup) flaked almonds
Icing (confectioners') sugar, to serve

1 Preheat the oven to 160°C (315°F/Gas 2–3). Put the cherries in a sieve set over a bowl and drain well, reserving the syrup.

2 Meanwhile, put the cream cheese, caster sugar, vanilla, egg and egg yolk in a food processor bowl and process until just combined, scraping down the side of the bowl occasionally. Add the flour and process until just combined. Take care not to overprocess the mixture.

3 Lightly brush a large baking tray with some of the melted butter. Lay the filo on a work surface and cover with a slightly damp tea towel (dish towel). Place one sheet of filo on the greased tray, brush well with butter and sprinkle with 1 tablespoon of the almond meal. Cover with another sheet of filo, brush with a little more butter and sprinkle with another tablespoon of almond meal *(pic 1)*. Continue layering with the remaining filo pastry, almond meal and butter — you should still have a little butter left at the end.

4 Use a rubber spatula to spread the cream cheese mixture down a long side of the pastry, about 5 cm (2 inches) in from the edge, to form a log shape. Press roughly one-quarter of the drained cherries gently into the mixture *(pic 2)*.

5 Carefully roll up the pastry to enclose the filling *(pic 3)*. Trim the edges of the strudel to neaten. Brush well with the remaining butter and sprinkle with the flaked almonds. Bake for 1 hour or until the pastry is crisp and deep golden and the filling is set. Cool on the tray.

6 Meanwhile, bring the reserved cherry syrup to the boil in a medium saucepan and simmer over medium–low heat for 15 minutes or until reduced by half and slightly syrupy. Remove from the heat, add the remaining cherries and cool.

7 To serve, use a serrated knife to slice the strudel. Serve dusted with icing sugar and with the cherries in the reduced syrup passed separately.

1

2

3

TIP Ready-made filo pastry is available both frozen and chilled. The chilled variety tends to be easier to handle and is less brittle than the frozen one. If using frozen filo, thaw it in the refrigerator overnight before using.

Conversion charts

OVEN TEMPERATURE		
°C	°F	Gas
70	150	1/4
100	200	1/2
110	225	1/2
120	235	1/2
130	250	1
140	275	1
150	300	2
160	315	2–3
170	325	3
180	350	4
190	375	5
200	400	6
210	415	6–7
220	425	7
230	450	8
240	475	8
250	500	9

LENGTH	
cm	inches
2 mm	1/16
3 mm	1/8
5 mm	1/4
8 mm	3/8
1	1/2
1.5	5/8
2	3/4
2.5	1
3	1 1/4
4	1 1/2
5	2
6	2 1/2
7	2 3/4
7.5	3
8	3 1/4
9	3 1/2
10	4
11	4 1/4
12	4 1/2
13	5
14	5 1/2
15	6
16	6 1/4
17	6 1/2
18	7
19	7 1/2
20	8
21	8 1/4
22	8 1/2
23	9
24	9 1/2
25	10
30	12
35	14
40	16
45	17 3/4
50	20

WEIGHT	
g	oz
5	1/8
10	1/4
15	1/2
20	3/4
30	1
35	1 1/4
40	1 1/2
50	1 3/4
55	2
60	2 1/4
70	2 1/2
80	2 3/4
85	3
90	3 1/4
100	3 1/2
115	4
120	4 1/4
125	4 1/2
140	5
150	5 1/2
175	6
200	7
225	8
250	9
280	10
300	10 1/2
350	12
375	13
400	14
450	1 lb
500	1 lb 2 oz
550	1 lb 4 oz
600	1 lb 5 oz
700	1 lb 9 oz
800	1 lb 12 oz
900	2 lb
1 kg	2 lb 3 oz

LIQUID	
ml	fl oz
30	1
60	2
80	2 1/2
100	3 1/2
125	4
160	5 1/2
185	6
200	7
250	9
300	10 1/2
350	12
375	13
400	14
500	17
600	21
650	22 1/2
700	24
750	26
800	28
1 L	35
1.25 L	44
1.5 L	52

Index

Q

R

S

T

U

V

W

Y

Z

Published in 2013 by Murdoch Books, an imprint of Allen & Unwin.

Murdoch Books Australia
83 Alexander Street
Crows Nest NSW 2065
Phone: +61 (0) 2 8425 0100
Fax: +61 (0) 2 9906 2218
www.murdochbooks.com.au
info@murdochbooks.com.au

Murdoch Books UK
Erico House, 6th Floor
93–99 Upper Richmond Road
Putney, London SW15 2TG
Phone: +44 (0) 20 8785 5995
Fax: +44 (0) 20 8785 5985
www.murdochbooks.co.uk
info@murdochbooks.co.uk

For Corporate Orders & Custom Publishing contact
Noel Hammond, National Business Development Manager,
Murdoch Books Australia

Publisher: Anneka Manning
Designers: Susanne Geppert and Robert Polmear
Photographers: Louise Lister, Julie Renouf, George Seper, Jared Fowler
Stylists: Kate Nixon, Marie-Helénè Clauzon, Jane Hann, Cherise Koch
Recipe Development: Sonia Greig, Leanne Kitchen, Cathie Lonnie, Anneka Manning, Lucy Nunes
Home Economists: Grace Campbell, Dixie Elliot, Joanne Glynn, Caroline Jones, Sharon Kennedy, Lucy Lewis, Sabine Spindler Allan Wilson
Production Manager: Karen Small

A cataloguing-in-publication entry is available from the catalogue of the National Library of Australia at www.nla.gov.au.

A catalogue record for this book is available from the British Library.

Printed by 1010 Printing International Limited, China

The Publisher and stylist would like to thank Breville (www.breville.com.au) for lending equipment for use and photography.

IMPORTANT: Those who might be at risk from the effects of salmonella poisoning (the elderly, pregnant women, young children and those suffering from immune deficiency diseases) should consult their doctor with any concerns about eating raw eggs.

OVEN GUIDE: You may find cooking times vary depending on the oven you are using. For fan-forced ovens, as a general rule, set the oven temperature to 20°C (35°F) lower than indicated in the recipe.

MEASURES GUIDE: We have used 20 ml (4 teaspoon) tablespoon measures. If you are using a 15 ml (3 teaspoon) tablespoon add an extra teaspoon of the ingredient for each tablespoon specified.